RUSSIA
AND
EUROPE

REINHARD WITTRAM

with 84 illustrations, 8 in color

HARCOURT BRACE JOVANOVICH, INC

Translated from the German by Patrick and Hanneluise Doran

Picture research by Alla Weaver

COPYRIGHT © 1973 THAMES AND HUDSON LTD, LONDON

First American edition 1973

ISBN 0–15–577963–X

Library of Congress Catalog Card Number: 72–91233

Printed in Great Britain by Jarrold and Sons Ltd, Norwich

CONTENTS

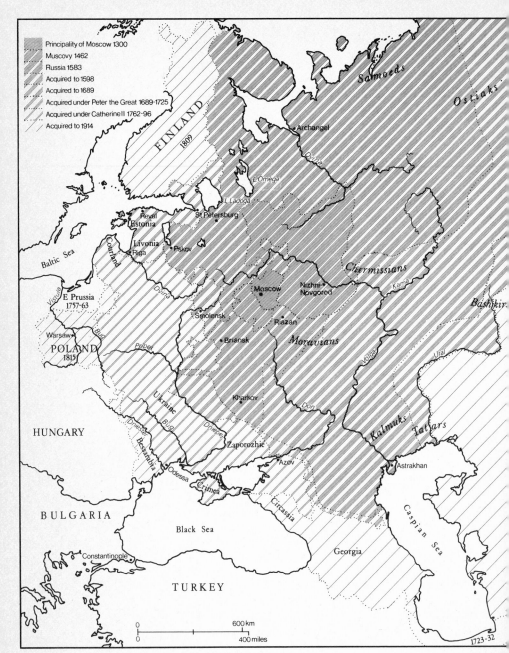

Legend:

- Principality of Moscow 1300
- Muscovy 1462
- Russia 1583
- Acquired to 1598
- Acquired to 1689
- Acquired under Peter the Great 1689-1725
- Acquired under Catherine II 1762-96
- Acquired to 1914

Samoeds

Ostiaks

FINLAND
1809

Archangel

Dvina

L.Omega

L.Ladoga

St Petersburg

Reval
Estonia

Livonia
Riga

Pskov

Courland

Dvina

Tchermissians

Kama

Baltic Sea

Moscow

Nizhni-
Novgorod

Bashkir

E Prussia
1757-63

Vistula

Bug

Smolensk

Riazan

Moravians

Volga

Ural

Warsaw

POLAND
1815

Pripet

Briansk

HUNGARY

Ukraine

Dniester

Bug

Dnieper

Kharkov

Don

Kalmuks

Tatars

Zaporozhie

Azov

Astrakhan

Bessarabia

Odessa

Crimea

Circassia

Caspian Sea

BULGARIA

Black Sea

Georgia

Constantinople

TURKEY

| 0 | | 600 km |
| 0 | | 400 miles |

1723-32

2 Expansion of Russia in Europe.

INTRODUCTION

Before embarking on a discussion of 'Russia' or 'Europe' the historian must make clear which period of history is under consideration. The 'Rus' of the ninth century had little in common with the 'Russe Common Wealth' about which Giles Fletcher wrote at the end of the sixteenth century while *Das veränderte Russland* (Reformed Russia) left behind by Peter the Great at his death in 1725 was as different from Fletcher's Muscovy as it was from the Imperial Russia of the year of revolution, 1917. To speak of Russia without bearing these differences in mind is to confuse; for during the course of a thousand years territorial boundaries have shifted, the social structure has altered and the cultural outlook has changed (it goes without saying that it must be kept in mind that the Russians have always been a European people and the Russian language a European language).

Europe, too, has changed, both in structure and in its own image. There is not, as yet, any consensus on its geographical limits. What is the dividing line between Europe and Asia? The Urals are not a boundary, either in a morphological or in a climatic sense, nor do they form an anthropo-geographical frontier. One nurtured in the Latin tradition and lacking any close ties with Russia might insist on three essential conditions for the 'true European', the 'complete European' – as did Paul Valéry in his lecture on the intellectual crisis at Zürich University in November 1922: 'Every race and land which has been successively Romanized, Christianized and conquered, in so far as the mind and teaching of the Greeks are concerned, is utterly European.' Experience of Roman civilization comes first. This point of view was as biased as that of Ranke to whom 'the Graeco-Slavonic principle' was effective in Russia only when it took on 'European forms'. Comparing Russia with Europe is easy, sterile and, indeed, unhistorical if the comparisons are between the earlier phases of Russian history and modern Europe, instead of stages of European development contemporaneous with the Russian ones.

In an address in September 1946 at the Rencontres Internationales de Genève on 'The European Spirit', Karl Jaspers sought to define it through three characteristics: 'the impulse to freedom', i.e. 'a conscious labour for the freedom of public conditions by means of the forms which shape the will in community', the consciousness of history rooted in freedom and the search for knowledge demanded by freedom. Several points arise here: absolutism with its despotic tendencies is also a phenomenon of European history, revolutionary movements wrenched from history are European as is the fear of knowledge and the persecution of critical and independent minds. It is understandable that the philosopher, as a Western European, could say in the same talk that Russia is physically near but distant in spirit (even when it attracts) while America though far away physically is so near in spirit as to be familiar. This remark must be examined concerning Russia.

Attempts similar to that of Jaspers have been made in that wild-goose chase to find the 'essence' of 'classical Europe', to understand 'European culture' (*Gesittung*) as an 'accepted moral code' and to see Europe's deeper meaning as the struggle for Freedom (W. Flitner). Federico Chabod in his *Storia dell'idea d'Europa* sought in 'Europe' a *forma mentis*, an attitude of mind, a moral consciousness. But these analyses always treat of modern Europe or a Europe seen in humanistic terms. Even the historian who restricts his researches to the more recent centuries has to be aware of conditions in earlier periods, just as he must take into consideration developments which do not correspond with his idea of the norm.

Such considerations demand that each historical phase must show in what way the social structure, the form of government, customs, events, ways of thinking and ideas of man in Russia are comparable with the rest of Europe and in what way they differ. It must be shown how Russia and Europe drifted apart and how, after long separation, they approached each other again. Much that seems to be 'typically European' may be identified in early Russia, though perhaps not at a similar phase of development or exactly in the same form. It is also possible that things that appear to be uniquely Russian contain European elements. If that is so they must not be brushed out of the European panorama.

Modern historians are wary of ideologies, and certainly they cannot allow themselves to be influenced either by Slavophile sympathies or Eurasian ideals, and they should be circumspect about attempts to cultivate European pride and to develop a normative ideology from some strong tendencies in ancient and modern European history.

I HIDDEN EUROPE

During the course of a few decades in the tenth and eleventh centuries Russia was in closer contact with Romano-German Europe than the Russian lands were to be at any other time during the succeeding five hundred years.

The few records extant are well known. The princely house of Rurik, Varangians who had become rapidly Slavicized and established in 'the great and wealthy principality' of Kiev on the Dnieper, made five or six marriage alliances with Western European ruling families during the latter half of the eleventh century. This does not take into account marriages with the royal houses of Sweden and Norway. A daughter of Great Prince Yaroslav the Wise married King Henry I of France in 1051, while one of his granddaughters (Eupraxia, Praxedis) became the second wife of Emperor Henry IV in 1089. Kiev and Regensburg were connected through a trade route.

Before this Western-oriented marriage policy was launched alliances of far-reaching consequence had been established with the imperial house at Constantinople. But Great Prince Vladimir of Kiev's acceptance of baptism from Byzantium brought no immediate break with Roman Christianity; some of the East-West marriages already referred to took place after the onset of the Great Schism in 1054, and there were numerous marriage alliances between members of the Roman Catholic Polish Piast dynasty and the Greek Orthodox house of Rurik as late as the twelfth and thirteenth centuries. In a survey of Kiev's relationship with Western Europe it has even been claimed 'that Russia was never more conscious of her common interests with Western Europe than in the period between the eleventh and thirteenth centuries, and this at a time when Europe stood in the greatest need of a friendly intermediary between the Latin and the Greek worlds' (F. Dvornik).

It was, in the long run, of crucial importance that Vladimir had not followed the example of his grandmother Olga who, it is presumed, had been baptized by missionaries from the Latin West and who had even requested clergy from Emperor Otto I.

All historical reflections about early Russia's relationship with the West must begin with the adherence of the Kievan 'Rus' to the Eastern Church. This led to a break with Latin Europe which lasted many centuries. Both churches, hostile to each other from the time of the Schism, developed along opposing lines and were never reunited. Again and again in later times Roman hopes for reunion were vainly centred in the Russian ruler who was, accordingly, wooed by the Roman authorities. Had a Russian great prince, tsar or emperor gone over to Rome and accepted papal supremacy over his Church, Russian-European relations would have developed in a very different way. But this separation of the churches was not the only factor in Russia's divergence from the West.

On the other hand the very self-reliance of the Russian Christian Church and her independence of Rome made it easier for her to approach the old European countries on a new basis in post-Reformation times. One has only to reflect on the frankness and remarkable biblical learning shown by Tsar Peter I in his theological discussions with the bishop of Salisbury, Gilbert Burnet, in England in 1698. The Christian syncretism of Alexander I – possible only because the Greek Orthodox emperor was not a member of the Catholic Church – was one of the most important aspects of his policy for European integration. And the close dynastic ties of the Russian imperial house with the Protestant princely families would have been hardly possible with a Catholic court.

Considering Russia's later expansion towards the East and her colonizing and missionary activity in Asia, her confessional separation from Latin Europe – itself split again by the Reformation – loses importance. Of much greater significance was the simple fact that the Russians had been Christian since the Middle Ages. On the whole, Russian Christianity was not un-European even though some Near Eastern pre-Christian mysticism seeped into its worship through Byzantium. In post-Reformation Europe the alien nature of Russian Christianity was sometimes strongly felt, while for centuries at a time the Russian Church shut itself off determinedly from all Western influences. At the present time those elements common to both traditions are being brought into focus by the ecumenical movement.

As yet, there exists no scientific comparative study of Western and Russian monasticism. From early beginnings and from the time of the earliest monastery still preserved, the Pecherskaya Lavra in Kiev (1051), about 550 monasteries were founded in Russia, mainly between the fourteenth and sixteenth centuries. Among these were wealthy, autonomous foundations owning vast estates, economically self-supporting and ruled over by influential abbots. Their number kept increasing, showing no appreciable decline up to the revolution despite much interference from the State. In 1914 there were more than a thousand monasteries and nunneries still in existence. How different these were from their Western counterparts can be seen from the following features: although Russian monasteries maintained schools and undertook educational work they rarely became centres of learning; a strong tradition of mysticism and asceticism, which invariably reasserted itself after periods of decline, was inherent in Russian monasticism and alongside the cenobitic life of the cloister the old eremitic tradition survived; assimilated into monasticism was the *starchestvo*, the institution of the father–confessor, spiritual director and teacher which was taken over from the Byzantine Church. At first intended for the young monks this institution came to exercise great influence on the laity. The most renowned of these monasteries, originally a hermitage, was Optina Pustyn in the Kaluga region. This was visited by many of the nineteenth century's leading intellectuals, among them Gogol, Dostoyevsky, Leo Tolstoy, Vladimir Soloviev and Konstantin Leontiev.

For the Western visitor to Russia one of the first indications of her alien nature was the style of her churches with their clusters of multi-coloured glittering cupolas. The prototype was, probably, the wooden palace chamber of the ruling dynasty in the pre-Christian period. From the Balkan Slavs to the Baltic, from Kiev and Vladimir to Novgorod and Pskov, and later in St Petersburg, various foreign architectural ideas were taken up and incorporated in these structures. As well as old stone buildings in the towns there were innumerable wooden churches – understandable in a country of vast forests. As the role of the Russian Church was essentially sacramental and liturgical rather than instructional, choral singing was of central importance in Orthodox worship.

More remarkable is the veneration of images: in icon painting with its strict stylistic canon both Byzantine and old oriental feeling for design show their influence. Is the icon an un-European element in Russia? An affirmative answer to this question would be of great

3 Detail of an eleventh-century fresco in St Sophia, Kiev.

4 Below, the Novodievitchy (New Virgin) Monastery for women, founded in 1524. The Regent Sophia, half-sister of Peter the Great, was obliged to enter this monastery in 1689. Engraving from Dixon Biancardi, *La Russia, da Tiflis a Stavropol*, 1877. British Museum.

5 St Sophia Cathedral (founded 1045) in the Novgorod Kremlin.

6 Below right, Cyril Belozersky, icon by Dionysus Glushitzky, 1424. Tretyakov Gallery, Moscow.

13

significance: for a thousand years the Russians were surrounded by these images day by day, from the cradle to the grave, both in their churches and in their homes. But it would be wrong to see in the icon either a heathen materialization of the divine or a deification of matter. Through the medium of the icon – so it has been said – the believer gazes upon the living face of the Saviour or of the Mother of God or of the Saints (S. Chetverikov). 'The icon makes manifest the tangible presence of God' (S. Bulgakov). And because man consists not only of soul and spirit but of body and matter the icon transmits the workings of the Spirit, i.e. miracles and blessings: therefore it is sacred and worthy of veneration. Although the representation of those portrayed is deeply stamped with the ascetic ideals of the Eastern Church, Russian iconography in its various periods was not just an imitation of Byzantine models. Iconographic research speaks of a 'progressive humanization of the aesthetic rules of form', of 'the gradual elimination of the magical elements'. Perhaps one can say that through art and man's feeling for life the Russian icon became Europeanized. Russia's greatest icon painter was Andrey Rublev (died *c.* 1425), a monk of the Troitsa-Sergieva monastery near Moscow, whose light effects and transparency of tone not only established him as supreme in Russia but raised him to the first rank in Western art (Onasch). Another critic rates Rublev's works as 'standing in a closer relationship to the genuine Greek tradition, by the subdued intensity of their composition, than the Italian paintings of the same period' (Weidlé).

Unlike the Roman Catholic Church the Russian Church did not interpret religion in a legalistic sense nor did it – like Protestantism – see the interpretation of the Word of God as its central task. Its primary concern was not dogma, nor hierarchic order nor theology but *sobornost*, κοινωνία, *communio*, the community rooted in love. The political implications of this will be discussed later.

This accords with a specifically Russian approach to the recognition of guilt. A comparable historical investigation would have to examine various penitential practices: the solemn public confessions of Ivan IV (The Terrible) in Moscow in 1550 and 1551; the general penitential services which the officiating patriarch, newly recalled from exile, held in 1607 during the Time of Troubles; Alexander I's handwritten draft of the principles of the Holy Alliance in 1815, with its clause calling for the moral improvement of rulers – vigorously expunged by Metternich. One recalls, too, how Maxim Gorky, a close friend of Lenin's, printed in his newspaper in 1917 a letter from a peasant demanding that the socialist press should not only settle accounts with the bourgeoisie but should take a strong line with its own failings. 'I salute this man', Gorky commented. 'Men of his type have a hard life, but leave behind an aura of great beauty.' While it is necessary to keep an open mind the question can be asked if the practice of self-criticism, introduced into Eastern Communist parties, is not a secularized form of Christian penitence? One thing is certain: with its inculcation of humility the Russian Church developed a unique form of European Christendom. But it was a European form which can only be understood in the context of the social and political history of Europe in which Russia, despite deep differences with the rest of the Continent, shared.

Paradoxical as it may seem the Russian Church showed her European character in what appeared to be her three most alien and repulsive traits: her tenacious superstition, her long-lasting intolerance and her dependence on the State.

Widespread superstition was closely linked to the educational backwardness of the people. Up to the outbreak of war in 1914 about 60 per cent of the adult population was illiterate. The country's first university was founded as late as 1755; by 1914 there were only nine. None of these had a theological faculty; the formation of clerics was undertaken by seminaries and four clerical academies. Educational backwardness was greatest among the peasantry. Nevertheless the Russian Church accomplished much in the field of elementary education from the end of the nineteenth century onwards. Here the situation was early European rather than un-European.

In one respect non-European habits of thought continued: from the Asiatic attitude to nature came the idea that man as a being composed of body and soul should not arbitrarily alter his appearance by cutting his hair or beard. When Peter the Great in 1698 tried to establish his new image of man with the order to shave, his instructions were not enforced against the clergy. As the peasantry was also allowed the wearing of beards an anthropological dualism established itself: peasants and clergy – the secular clergy, who were invariably married, as well as the monks and the episcopacy – continued an archaic custom shot through with mythological and superstitious elements.

Intolerance was based not only on foundations similar to those obtaining in all Christian denominations up to the wars of religion

15

and beyond but also on the old Orthodox theological teaching that Church and State formed a unity like body and soul and were indivisible. The practical tolerance of other creeds, even non-Christian ones, which was already the norm in Moscow in the seventeenth century precluded neither proselytizing nor the primacy of the State Church which obtained up to the fall of the monarchy. Only after the Toleration Edict of 1905 was withdrawal from membership of the Russian Orthodox Church not punishable as desertion. The persecution of heretics was also known in Russia, especially during the opposition to Western influences in the sixteenth century. Nor was the persecution of old Orthodox Russian schismatics and legal discrimination against them brought to an end by Peter the Great's principles of toleration. Considering the confessional politics of Catholic Spain, whose inclusion in Europe is unquestionable, the continuous pressure exerted by the Russian State even into the twentieth century against all those who, although claimed as faithful by the Orthodox Church, wished to withdraw from it, seems just another chapter of European ecclesiastical history.

In conclusion the relationship between Church and State in Russia is only a special example of the political uncertainties of European Christendom. When the Muscovite Great Prince Ivan III (1462–1505), who had been married to a niece of the last Byzantine emperor in 1472, drew up the Russian coronation statutes in 1498 on the Byzantine model, an important distinction was made: the great prince, who was not called Basileus remained without religious functions and without the acclamation of holiness. In spiritual matters he was subordinate to the Church. It is not correct, therefore, to label the Russian monarchic system as Caesaropapism. What is correct is that the ruler claimed, acquired and retained absolute power. This theory was given a theological foundation by Abbot Joseph of Volokolamsk (died 1515) who taught that as it was the duty of the ruler to protect the Orthodox faith and to defend the Church he was responsible for its every member and could fulfil this duty only if all power was in his hands. This included complete authority in ecclesiastical affairs. In unsuccessful opposition to this was a group of hermits and monks (Nil Sorskii, Prince Patrikeev) who upheld the principle of poverty and the independence of the Church from State interference.

When the Patriarchate was established in Moscow in 1589 it was 'a work of the State' (Stökl). The Muscovite patriarch was raised to

7 The patriarch touches the bowed head of the tsar during the Feast of the Trinity in Red Square, Moscow. Engraving from *Vermehrte newe Moskowitische und Persianische Reise*, 1635–36 by Adam Olearius (1656 edition). British Museum.

his office by the 'wish' of the tsar and at the 'request' of the Church Assembly, the *sobor*. In the seventeenth century two important patriarchs, Philaret (1618–33), the great-grandfather of Peter the Great and Nikon (1652–58) achieved a position of power ranking equally with that of the ruler. In principle Peter the Great, who replaced the Patriarchate with the Holy Synod, introduced nothing new; for the ruler's ultimate authority in Church affairs was never brought into dispute and the imperial reformer had no ambition to be spiritual head of the Church. But, through bureaucracy and increasing State influence, Peter was largely responsible for the loss of political power by the Church. Such a development was no different from that in other European states. The purposive State-Church policy of the influential Chief Procurator K. P. Pobedonostsev (1880–1905), based on religious zeal, was even in Russia generally felt to be an anachronism. However it must be mentioned that reform tendencies did come into play in the Russian Church after 1905, among them a demand for greater independence from the State. The fall of the monarchy in the February Revolution in 1917 was not condemned by the Holy Synod; on the contrary it welcomed the 'hour of Freedom'.

Looking back over the whole field of Russian history one should not place too much emphasis on a theory drawn up at the beginning of the sixteenth century; the doctrine propounded by the monk Philotheus of Pskov that Moscow was the third Rome, not to be followed by a fourth. That the hopes of Orthodox Christendom turned towards the source of Russian power after the fall of Constantinople (1453) is not surprising. The scholarly monk, who in 1510 appealed to the Muscovite Great Prince Basil III, elucidated a great vision of a 'New Rome', which was to be the last. His purpose was to warn the ruler to protect and cherish Orthodoxy. While this historico-theological speculation might be fascinating for a student of history it exercised no influence on the sober power-politics of the Muscovite and St Petersburg governments.

Russia's most significant withdrawal from Western Europe was brought about by the territorial shift of the centre of princely power from Kiev and the Dnieper valley via Suzdal and Vladimir to Moscow. The development of various new centres of power was a result of the so-called 'brother's law' of the princely family, a special form of seniority necessitating subdivisions which led to quarrels. The opportunities which the undeveloped forests of the north-east offered as regions for forest clearance and colonization also played a part. During the impressive colonizing process, generally regarded as one of the most important developments in Russian history, the Great Russian people came into existence. Moscow – first mentioned in 1147 – became their capital. Unlike other towns, e.g. Polotsk, Smolensk, Vladimir, Tver, Moscow's existence owed nothing to natural trade routes. Its rise between 1400 and 1600 had other causes, its importance as a trading centre coming later than its choice as a political capital.

Although Moscow was much further away from the Latin West – counting travelling time – than Kiev or Novgorod the rivalry between the appanage princes resulted in the creation of a buffer zone which became an increasingly strong barrier because of the development of the Lithuanian-Russian Empire. Olgerd, son of the Lithuanian Great Prince Gedymin (who died in 1341) and twice married to princesses of the Rurik dynasty, reached the gates of Moscow in his campaigns of 1368 and 1370–71. Various truces confirmed his suzerainty over a number of Russian appanage princes. When Olgerd's son Jagiello was

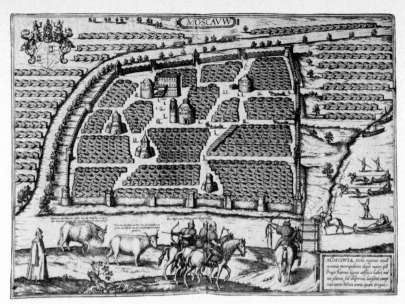

8 Moscow, with the Kremlin (fortress) in the centre, in the sixteenth century. Engraving from Braun und Hohenburg, *Orbis Terrarum*, 1570. British Museum.

baptized a Roman Catholic in 1386 and then married the Polish Queen Jadwiga and was crowned king of Poland, a union was established giving a wide power basis to the religious differences. The *terrae Russiae* from Breslau and Kiev in the south to Briansk, Mosalsk and Toropec in the east and north became part of the Polish-Lithuanian Union. So did the principality of Smolensk, which because of its position between Moscow and Poland-Lithuania was fought for again and again. After a short period of independence Smolensk passed to Poland-Lithuania in 1404, in 1514 it went to Moscow, back to Poland in 1611 and finally to Moscow in 1654.

At this period the notion developed along the whole border zone which was made up of the Polish kingdom and Livonia – itself Protestant since the Reformation – that here was the outer bastion of Christianity. Poland took this metaphor unto itself, with a glance towards the schismatic East. In a humanistic ode of 1595 Riga, at that time subject to the king of Poland, was lauded as 'the bulwark against Moscow', and alongside Vienna, the champion against the Turks, was seen as 'Europe's other sword'. In Moscow, on the other hand, the Latin drive for power and the exercise of that power was seen as a danger to Orthodoxy, the only true faith.

Perhaps the opposition would not have developed such sharpness if Russia had not been conquered and laid under tribute by the Mongols (the Tartars) in 1237–40. Ryazan was the first to fall, followed by all the princely centres and towns from Kolomna and Moscow to Tver and Torzhok and in the south to Kiev. Only Novgorod remained exempt. Before 1239–40 the West had no intimation of the Mongol threat. At the very time when the Mongols with their massed cavalry and their Chinese techniques of conquest were swarming across Russia towards the West, Emperor Frederick II was winning the help of European rulers in his struggle for northern Italy. Although Pope Gregory IX appealed for a crusade against the Tartars in 1239, his call was as ineffectual as the emperor's. And when the Mongols, in the spring of 1241, swept simultaneously into Silesia and Hungary the West was unable to defend itself.

Russian historians have recorded with bitterness that in 1240 Swedes from Finland and the Teutonic Order from Livonia invaded Russian territory and that hard-pressed Greek Orthodoxy was stabbed in the back by Roman Catholic Christianity. The defence of Orthodoxy fell to the prince of Novgorod, Alexander, called Nevsky since his victory over the Swedes on the Neva. He defeated the Teutonic Knights on the frozen Lake Peipus in 1242 and compelled them to renounce further conquests at the conclusion of peace in 1243. Alexander, afterwards prince of Kiev and great prince of Vladimir, was forced to recognize Tartar overlordship, like all other Russian princes. He was later canonized by the Russian Church. But his military and religious fame came not from the defence of Christendom against the heathen but from a victory over the Christian enemies of Orthodoxy.

It is difficult to estimate the significance for Russia of almost two hundred years of Tartar rule. It meant, above all, the exaction of tribute but it was also a political overlordship, for the Russian princes and great princes were, without exception, nominated by the Tartars and were under the necessity of purchasing their office by presents and by personal appearance in the Golden Horde, the khan's army base at Sarai on the Lower Volga. In the first hundred years the foreign despot became arbitrator in the disputes of the Russian princely dynasties, which was humiliating enough. Later on the collection of the tribute and its payment to the khan became the monopoly of Great Prince Ivan I (Kalita) of Moscow (1328–41). This was the beginning of Moscow as the new centre of Russian power. By forcing the appanage princes to relinquish their own relationship with the Golden Horde the great prince concentrated into his own hands the advocacy of Russian interests with the khan. Step by step he acquired control over the other principalities by promising protection and by demanding services. With the support of the khans he changed the law of succession: gradually and with lasting effect he substituted primogeniture for seniority, without entirely destroying the appanages. Most likely, too, it was because of Moscow's claim to sole representation that there was little direct contact between Russians and Tartars, divided as they were by religious differences. Yet in spite of this it must be accepted that foreign rule had both direct and indirect consequences.

A number of phrases, derived most probably from gestures of submission and forms of obeisance used in relations with the Tartar khans, were borrowed by colloquial Russian and legal terminology. The touching of the head or forehead, an oriental gesture of submissiveness comes to mind. This went beyond the liturgical Proskynese. *Chelom bit'*, *chelobit'e*, *chelobitnaya*, which have long lost their literal meaning, preserved the memory of the practice which compelled even princes to touch the ground with their foreheads before the potentate. But the Mongol Empire came not just with brute force but with old cultural forms, worthy of imitation. These, from distant places such as Central Asia and Egypt, were assimilated and handed on; various engineering skills, the art of administration,

9 The characteristic deep obeisance to the tsar is seen in this Easter Festival procession. Engraving from *Voyages du Sieur Adam Olearius*, 1635–36 (1718 edition, Leyden).

especially in the field of finance management, and sophisticated means of communication. The State postal service, which made travel over vast distances within the empire possible, has been described as 'one of the most brilliant institutions of the empire' (Spuler). The Russians became so accustomed to sovereignty as exercised on a vast territorial scale that they turned their eyes towards Asia and were diverted from Western Europe.

The power of compulsion was, of course, more effective than the prospects of assimilation. The religious tolerance of the Tartars was responsible for the relationship between 'Russia' and 'Europe'. When John of Plano Carpini, Innocent IV's Franciscan emissary to the great khan, returned in 1247 he reported that the foreign ruler was planning a new campaign against the West and that he demanded the allegiance of Latin rulers. But he also brought back the information that many Nestorian Christians had influence at the court of the khan. The Golden Horde had not only not suppressed the Russian Church but had protected and favoured it, exempting it from the payment of tribute. Nor did this state of affairs change in the thirteenth century when the Tartars were reluctantly converted to Islam. A Greek Orthodox bishopric was established in Sarai for those Russians who had settled there. Neither side attempted to proselytize, so no crusading zeal was generated. Later on when armed strife did occur the Church, as was to be expected, blessed the crusade. The victory of the great prince of Moscow, Dmitri (Donskoi) over the Emir Mamai on the field of Kulikovo (the snipefield) on the Upper Don in 1380 made an ineradicable impression on the Russian mind. 'Never was their own Christianity and therefore their non-Asiatic nature so clearly demonstrated to the Russian people as during this period, which is so often cited as evidence of their Asiatic character' (Irene Neander).

To contrast the effects of Islam on two of Europe's most remote corners, Russia and Spain, would be an interesting and instructive exercise in European history. But Mongol power in eastern Russia cannot be compared with the advanced culture of the Arabs in Spain. The Tartar Mohammedans have influenced neither science nor art. It is easy to speculate that if they had had a more advanced non-Christian culture it might have been dangerous for the European character of Russia. But under an outward show of dependence the substance was preserved. It is probably true to say that the Christian Church with its hierarchy and monasteries, its liturgy and art was the strongest force in the preservation of the singularly European character of the Great Russians, harassed as they were from both East and West.

From the second decade of the fifteenth century the empire of the Golden Horde was in decline: in 1438 the khanate of Kazan broke away, followed in 1449 by the khanate of the Crimea. But this did not put an end to the Tartar threat to Russia; for Tartar suzerainty gave way to Tartar expeditions of plunder (reflected in the Russian proverb that 'an uninvited guest is worse than the Tartars'). At the same time, however, it won for the great prince of Moscow some political elbow-room which allowed a systematic increase in his own power. How much the power ratio shifted in Moscow's favour from the end of the fourteenth century can be judged by the large numbers of the Tartar upper class who entered Russian service, became Christian and were assimilated by the Russian nobility. In all about 130 families

10 Church art continued to flourish while Russia was subject to the Tartars. As seen in this icon painting, *St George and the Dragon*, Novgorod School, early fifteenth century. Tretyakov Gallery, Moscow.

became Russified, among them were names like Apraksin, Naryshkin, Saburov, Turgenev, Uvarov. In this was shown the Europeanizing strength of the Moscow State, which, in conquering the khanates of Kazan (1552) and Astrakhan (1556), extended its authority into the innermost territories of the former Mongol Empire.

Recent research has shown that neither the social structure of ancient Russia nor its governmental system can be dismissed as un-European. Each must be examined as objectively as possible, eschewing ideological pre-conceptions.

It has been demonstrated most convincingly that during the Muscovite period social conditions were similar to those prevailing in early Europe, but they survived in their archaic form for a longer period in Russia. A distinctive characteristic which differentiated Russian peasants from other European rural communities was their high degree of mobility: peasants lived not only from tillage – often just primitive 'out-field' exploitation – but from fishing and forestry as well, so that in a migratory process lasting hundreds of years they opened up the vast forests of European Russia. In appanage Russia the peasantry was subject to many laws, varying from one dependency to another; there were also groups of bonded peasants and various categories of dependence. As late as 1497 the right of migration was unchallenged, still formally accepted in the First Sudebnik, Ivan III's legal code, Article 57 of which allowed peasants to change their place of employment only once a year, on 26 November, the Feast of St George (*Yur'ev den'*).

A hundred years later political and economic pressures were leading to peasant bondage both to the land and the landlord, thereby laying the foundations of fully fledged serfdom. The gradual abolition of the right of migration resulted in the illegal flight of peasants, which, in turn, led to discriminatory edicts. By an ukaz of Tsar Fyodor Ivanovich of 1597 absconding peasants could be reclaimed only within five years of their escape. In 1607 the right of migration was completely abolished, without bringing the movement of peasants to a halt. Even the legal code (*Ulozhenie*) of Tsar Alexei Mikhailovich of 1649 (the Second Sudebnik) brought no change in that situation. From then on the peasant's bondage to the soil was absolute. No longer were runaway peasants protected by any term of limitation; nevertheless the State was forced to counter peasant abscondence by constant decrees. In opposition to the encroachment of the State the peasant revolts occurred. Historically, bondage and the desire for liberty were linked together in Russia.

The regulatory prescriptions of the *mir*, the village commune, were as important for the destiny and self-awareness of the Russian peasant as the development of the so-called law of bondage, abolished as late as 1861. Only in the nineteenth century, through the studies of Freiherr von Haxthausen, was it discovered that this Russian institution was unique in Europe. It must be said straight away that, because of special circumstances, corporate solidarity as known in other European countries found its Russian counterpart neither among the nobility nor in burgher guilds but among the peasantry. Discarding both myth and obsolete theories it remains true to say that the Russian agricultural commune, the *mir*, came into existence in the Middle Ages not as a property-co-operative, or land-collective, but as a unit of communal liability. In a Novgorodian version of *Russkaya Pravda*, the legal code of the eleventh–twelfth century, the word – used in a technical sense – referred to communal responsibility for crimes committed within the territory of the commune and it was still being used in this general sense in the fourteenth century. Later on the *mir*, as a communal gathering, had the function of regulating labour-burdens among the free State peasants as well as among State serfs and landlords' serfs. Of course the extent and importance of this form of self-government varied according to region and social conditions. In the course of a radical change in production techniques – the slow movement of agriculture towards a market economy from the sixteenth century onwards – and in conjunction with other changes the *mir* became transformed into an organization for the redistribution of communal land during the eighteenth century. This meant, in effect, that it came to regulate the equal distribution of land holdings as well as of obligations.

The paramount importance of the *mir* has been attested by many commentators. In spite of its narrowly defined area of competence this can be seen – from a socio-psychological point of view – as the emergence of certain behaviour patterns: the habit of communal responsibility, the ability for self-help and the organization of communal welfare.

This tendency in the Russian people was strengthened by the very old institution of the *artel*. This was a voluntary association set up for

11 An illumination from the MS of Skazanie o Mamaevom Poboishche depicting the bloody encounter between Prince Vladimir Andreevich and his troops and the Emir Mamai and his Tartars. British Museum.

economic purposes which organized communal services and work. In this way the participants provided for themselves a co-operative organization under their own control. The word is Turkish in origin. In Russia the *artel* developed in many different forms, sometimes temporarily, sometimes permanently because of economic needs. *Arteli* existed among land-workers, everywhere in the fishing trade, in the peasant cottage industries, among itinerant craftsmen, and in the building and transport trades. 'A medieval impulse to join in small groups for communal work lasted longer among the Russians than any other people. Forty years ago Kropotkin could regard the *artel* – itself one of the peculiar social set-ups to arise from this impulse – as the essence of the Russian peasants' way of life' (Martin Buber, 1946/50).

To this two points should be added. Considering the strength and variety of voluntary corporate structures, especially in the largest social class, the peasantry, Russia should be compared with Europe in a much deeper sense than geography and ethnography would suggest. Furthermore, the rapid, independent formation of the Russian worker

26

12 Alexander Nevsky (1236–65), the great Russian heroic figure, was canonized by the Church for his defence of Orthodoxy. Commemorative fresco from the cathedral of Archangel Michael, Moscow Kremlin. >

councils in 1905 and the worker, soldier and peasant councils in 1917 would be incomprehensible if the old habit of communal deliberation and united action were unknown to Russian history.

The most striking un-European element in Russian society was the absence of a free, self-regulating middle-class community, the non-existence of the *Bürger*, the *bourgeois*, the 'citizen', but this was nothing more than the perpetuation of early European conditions. Like many early medieval towns in the rest of Europe numerous Russian towns developed under the protection of a princely burg (the *kreml*) as a suburb (the *posad*) to which were adjoined some privileged residential quarters ('liberties', *slobody*). Later, in the fifteenth and sixteenth centuries, numerous villages attained the status of towns thanks to their favourable positions on trade routes. One must suppose that Tartar rule hindered or even stopped the development of international trade and with it a self-reliant burgher class. A town such as Novgorod which remained outside the area dominated by the Golden Horde became a strong middle-class community. At the same time the special conditions and circumstances of the whole of Russian economic production must be examined.

Distances, climate and transport conditions explain why the Russian peasant had to be, to a great extent, his own craftsman. The transition from peasant to craftsman was an easy one. The merchant

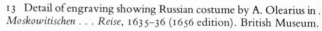

13 Detail of engraving showing Russian costume by A. Olearius in . *Moskowitischen . . . Reise*, 1635–36 (1656 edition). British Museum.

14 Muscovite merchants pulling their boat overland between rivers Woodcut from Olaus Magnus, *Historia delle genti delle cose Settentrionali*, Venice, 1656.

did not export highly specialized manufactured goods but raw materials or semi-manufactured articles (furs, pelts and leather, honey and wax, flax and hemp). Economically he was bound more strongly to a rural catchment area than to a guildsman. The 'decisive difference' between the structure of the Russian town compared with its counterpart in the rest of Europe has been seen by the social historian O. Brunner as the absence of long-distance trade and export business. The Russian town never acquired jurisdictional independence. Town and country never became legally distinct. The German proverb 'Stadtluft macht frei' (town air confers freedom) was irrelevant in Russian conditions. The peasant who moved into a town to follow a trade remained tied to his village community and to his landlord. True the tax-paying townspeople, the tradesmen as well as the long-distance merchants, were grouped into separate corporations, into tax and service communes with their own offices, assembly halls and chancelleries. But – with the exception of Novgorod – they did not form political entities. A characteristic function of these corporations was the office held by the *tselovalnik*, a juror elected by the tax-paying community who through kissing (*tselovatj*) the Cross was sworn in and made responsible as treasurer and tax collector in the service of the public treasury.

Even the economically strongest group, the wholesale merchants who were divided into three guilds – and for whom the title 'guests' (*gosti*), used also during the Middle Ages in Europe, was maintained – was bound directly to the State administration. These merchants were used as the porters and servants of the princes. The historical consequences of the Russian foreign trade groups were important: through their enterprise and initiative, their accumulation of capital and their far-ranging contacts they contributed substantially to the development and stabilization of the Russian home market. But they did not form a political entity; they lacked the power to achieve autonomy, and there was no question of anyone in Russia being able to acquire exemption from taxation.

As already mentioned conditions were different in Novgorod (also in Pskov). In this oligarchic city-state generations of landowning boyars together with representatives of the merchants and the assembly of the old Russian residential quarter (*vyeche*) ruled, and the elected prince was reduced to the status of a hired captain. Novgorod the Great which, next to the great principality of Moscow, ruled over the

15 The great city of Novgorod which rivalled Moscow in importance till its independence was lost to Ivan III at the end of the fifteenth century. Eighteenth-century coloured broadsheet.

largest territory of old Russia, as far north as the White Sea, was in direct commercial link with the Western world. The most visible sign of its commercial and political links with the west was St Peter's, the strictly demarcated enclave of the Hanseatic League in Novgorod. The end of its freedom and, at the same time, the change in its relationship with the West was brought about by the Muscovite Great Prince Ivan III who after subduing Pskov in 1460 gained control of Novgorod in 1478–79. Its political independence was abolished and the *vyeche* bell taken to Moscow, Church lands and private estates were expropriated and the resettlement of the leading burghers in the interior of Russia was begun. In a series of actions lasting up to 1488 the basis of Novgorod's independence was destroyed. By 1499 three-quarters of all ecclesiastical lands had been secularized, while the Hansa office there had been closed since 1494.

As far as foreign policy was concerned the incorporation of Novgorod and its dependent regions into the Muscovite principality

6 *The Trinity*, 1422–27, icon painting by Andrey Rublev (1370–1430). Tretyakov Gallery, Moscow.

had far-reaching consequences. The rule of the great princes and tsars now reached as far as the northern coastline and included, in the Neva region, a small section of the Baltic coast without harbours. Moscow acquired as neighbours Swedish Finland and the ecclesiastical territories in Livonia which belonged to the Teutonic Order, the bishopric of Dorpat and the archbishopric of Riga, all part of the Holy Roman Empire. An army consisting of Russians from Moscow, Pskov and Novgorod invaded Livonia for the first time in 1481. When concluding a ten-year peace the Livonians were forced to accept the formula *dobisha chelom*, the phrase with which they expressed their homage. The Hansa towns were forced to include the same formula in their peace treaty with the Russians in 1487. Opposite the fortress of the Teutonic Order near Narva Ivan III erected in 1492 the stone fortress of Ivangorod.

From this time onwards the proximity of Russia to this border area of Western Christendom was seen as a danger. Although the Livonian master of the Teutonic Order gained a military victory over the Russians in 1502 south of Pskov on the Smolina lake the political situation remained uncertain; for the Muscovite great prince and tsar granted to the Livonians only limited armistices, humiliating in form and dangerous in content, and since 1509 disguised as a 'clemency', i.e. with the very same terminology as used for pardoned subjects. The territorial encroachment of Moscow on this distant corner of Romano-German Europe at first caused only apprehension in her neighbours.

The form of government of the Muscovite great princes and tsars, as observed and described by foreign visitors to Russia, contributed

17 Wolter von Plettenberg, Master of the Teutonic Order in Livonia, 1494–1535. Statue in the castle courtyard, Riga.

18 Narva, coastal town in Livonia, with the fortress of the early Teutonic Order and the Russian fortress of Ivangorod. Eighteenth-century engraving, British Museum.

not a little to their impression of strangeness. One of the earliest and most impressive authors to present a survey of Muscovite affairs to the rest of Europe was the imperial envoy Freiherr Siegmund von Herberstein, who was in Moscow in 1517 and 1526. In his account of his travels *Rerum Moscoviticarum commentarii* (first published in 1549), he described Muscovite rule as a form of tyranny: the power of the great prince over his subjects surpassed that of any other ruler in the world, their lives and possessions completely at his service. Not one of his advisers would dare to hold an opinion contrary to his, let alone oppose him. 'Fatentur publice voluntatem principis Dei esse voluntatem' (They profess publicly that the will of the prince is the will of God). 'Gens illa magis servitute quam libertate gaudet' (These people derive more happiness from slavery than from freedom).

Herberstein's statements cannot be accepted without reservations, as will be seen later on. But Muscovite rule was, without doubt, both autocratic and monocratic. In explaining the development of Muscovite autocracy (*samoderzhavie*) the following circumstances must be taken into account: in those territories deforested and colonized by the Russians each principality was founded by a prince, his family and his retainers, thereby turning it into a hereditary estate (*votchina*). In his treaties with the other appanage princes the Muscovite great prince was always able to bind the princely families more closely to himself. How the appanage princes lost their power and were politically emasculated, not without the connivance of the khan, has been already mentioned. In Russian historical writing this process is known as 'the gathering of the Russian Lands'. Many princes and their brothers, sons, cousins and nephews were drawn gradually into the service of the Muscovite great princes and in this way became

33

their vassals (boyars). Out of a total of about two hundred Muscovite boyars in the sixteenth century about 130 held the title of prince (Klyuchevsky). From the fifteenth century onwards more and more voyars of the appanage princes entered the service of the great prince, at first retaining the 'right of departure' and the right to change service. But the great princes gradually withdrew these rights by demanding guarantees and by confiscating the boyar's land should he leave the service of the great princes without permission. As more and more appanage principalities became absorbed in Muscovy fewer opportunities for alternative service remained to the boyars. Service contracts were replaced by vassalage. During the fifteenth century the title of 'tsar' was introduced into Moscow quite independently of the connection with Byzantium. 'The autocracy of the great prince of Moscow was firmly established before he pronounced himself to be the heir of the Greek Autokrator' (Stökl). The Byzantine tradition did not produce Russian autocracy, but confirmed it. Ivan III's marriage to the niece of the last Byzantine emperor, a girl who grew up in Italy, brought Italian rather than Greek influences to Moscow, as can be seen in Muscovite architecture. The title 'tsar', of doubtful origin etymologically, soon afterwards – through its translation into *Kaiser* in a treaty with the Emperor Maximilian I in 1514 – gave the Russian ruler the opportunity to secure for himself the supreme dignity.

In this system of government there was no room for representative institutions. There was, of course, the traditional council of boyars, the Duma, an advisory council to the princes and great princes. Its composition and convocation was at the discretion of the ruler, but during the Mongol period it had been an influential body. The Great Prince Dmitri Donskoi (died 1389) was credited with having attached importance to the co-operation of the council of boyars. Great Prince Vassily, Ivan III's son and father of Ivan IV, appears to have been the first to act as an autocrat, relying only on one or two trusted advisers. In spite of this one hesitates to see in this the Western idea of absolutism; for in Moscow autocracy was actual power, theologically interpreted, not a development from late Roman jurisprudence. That the boyars with their pre-ordained claims to place and rank had still some importance Ivan IV, The Terrible, discovered during his younger days. Many of his later measures can be seen as an attempt to destroy the corporate basis of boyar power.

II FROM MOSCOW TO ST PETERSBURG

The beginnings of Russia's relationship with the other European states in modern times must be sought not in Peter the Great's reforms and his new base on the Baltic but in Muscovy, slowly expanding though not yet fully stabilized, in the concerns of her neighbours and the unavoidable fluidity of her frontiers.

From the end of the fifteenth century Poland's enemies were particularly interested in forging links with Muscovy, especially the grand master of the Teutonic Order in Prussia and the emperor in Vienna, who was Livonia's nominal suzerain. Naturally Prussia and Livonia differed in their attitude towards Russia: Russian pressure was neither so strong nor so immediate in Königsberg as it was in Dorpat and Riga. Livonia, therefore, was more inclined than Prussia to look to Poland-Lithuania as an ally against Muscovy.

With Muscovy's growing sense of power during the reign of Ivan III went the need to acquire the technical expertise and to recruit the specialists on which the military and cultural supremacy of the West was based. It has already been noted how the Italian architects who enlarged the Kremlin for Ivan III brought a breath of the Renaissance to Moscow. But the shortest and most popular route to Muscovy from Central and Western Europe was via the Baltic and through the borderlands of Livonia. While the Muscovites were intent on securing imports of military equipment and the immigration of munition workers the Teutonic Order in Livonia, as the neighbouring power most endangered by this traffic, tried to close those routes which were under its control. On the conclusion of yet another truce between Muscovy and Livonia in 1554 one of the Russian conditions was that through-trade to Russia was not to be interfered with and that no alliance was to be made with Poland-Lithuania. When the Livonians broke this agreement in 1557 the tsar began the ensuing war with the aim of conquering Livonia, a country which was alien to Muscovy in religion, race, law and politics.

The Livonian War, which dragged on for almost a quarter of a century, ended with the exhaustion of Muscovy, the abandonment of the tsar's claims on Livonia and the extension of the power of Poland and Sweden. Despite this it can hardly be claimed that Muscovy

19 The harbour of Reval in Estonia, under German magistracy (thirteenth century to 1905) with German-style architecture; 1561–1710 under Swedish domination. Engraving by A. Olearius in . . . *Moskowitischen* . . . *Reise* (1656 edition). British Museum.

was, as a result, any further removed from the West than before. It is true that during the Reformation period Church and State in Muscovy eliminated all heretical tendencies coming in from the West; the conquest of the two Tartar khanates on the Volga diverted part of Russia's energy eastwards; Tartar auxiliaries in the Muscovite army added to its alien image; finally the gloomy and neurotic Tsar Ivan IV (1547–84), whose Russian sobriquet *Grozny* only later acquired a pejorative meaning in the other main European languages (The Terrible, *Der Schreckliche*, *Le Terrible*), was so unpredictable during the latter part of his life that he intimidated and terrified those who came in contact with him. The historian must not, of course, overlook the fact that about the same time as Ivan Grozny with the help of his black-clad political police, the *oprichniki*, was repeatedly dealing out savage punishment to his enemies, the St Bartholomew's Day Massacre was being organized in Paris and the duke of Alba was setting up his oppressive regime in the Spanish Netherlands.

There is no doubt that the tsar's invasion of Livonia caused the greatest alarm. Many saw him as a tyrant. But at the same time this tsar as no other before him aroused the curiosity of his European contemporaries, fascinating them by his extraordinary behaviour. His great ability and his strange fantasies were notorious. Jan Rocyta, a Protestant preacher accompanying a Polish embassy to Moscow and an elder of the Bohemian Brotherhood, engaged him in a public religious disputation in 1570, in which the tsar analysed, with theological acuteness, the weaknesses of Protestantism. Those English travellers and envoys who made his acquaintance noted his undisguised piety as well as his 'strange spirit', his intelligence and – after he had mortally wounded his eldest son in a sudden fit of rage – his 'extreme griefe'. For them his failings had all the ingredients of high tragedy. Generally speaking Russia at the end of the sixteenth century appeared to Englishmen as a strange, outlandish and barbarous land, Christian, to be sure, but part-European, part-Asiatic.

During the Livonian War Ivan IV gained political as well as military successes: in spite of his deportation of the bourgeoisie of Dorpat and numerous other Livonians to Russia in 1565 he found followers in Livonia among a small group of German nobles. However, the two noblemen who entered his service (Taube and Kruse) and who together with two other Germans even joined the *oprichniki* soon afterwards forsook the tsar and betrayed him. In the same way it was of no lasting consequence that Duke Magnus of Holstein, brother of the king of Denmark, who was created king of Livonia in 1570 as a Russian vassal and was married soon afterwards to a Russian princess, abandoned the tsar in 1578 and placed himself under the protection of the king of Poland. Already then many Western Europeans were entering the service of Muscovy, either on a short-term or a permanent basis.

At two strategic points a new connection with the Western world opened up for Muscovy: briefly at Narva, for a longer time on the White Sea.

20 Contemporary icon portrait of Ivan IV. Nationalmuseum, Copenhagen.

From May 1558 to September 1581 Narva was under Russian rule. Many merchants from *entrepôts* in the West travelled to Narva to trade in the Russian market. From Narva the first Russian naval vessels, built and manned by Englishmen, sailed the Baltic. One cannot, of course, speak yet of Russian sea power. The tsar was unable to gain control of the two great harbours of Reval and Riga, and Muscovy took no part in the Swedish-Danish rivalry for the *Dominium maris Baltici*.

The opening of the northern sea route by the English was of the greatest importance. The events are so well known that a few sentences will suffice: Competing against Spain and Portugal for overseas sources of raw materials an English squadron sought a northern route to China in 1553; the expedition failed but a ship under the command of Richard Chancellor accidentally found the mouth of the Northern Dvina. On the strength of a report from Chancellor, who was received in Moscow by the tsar, the Muscovy Company was founded in London in February 1555. In the same year it received a Russian trading licence. In 1567 a second licence gave the English sole trading rights on the White Sea and a further one in 1569 gave them the monopoly of the maritime transit-trade with Persia.

Commercially the connection with Russia was not of much importance to England. The number of ships which sailed yearly to northern Russia was small (five or six), their tonnage insignificant (not more than a total of 700 tons). The most important item of naval stores which England bought from Russia was rigging. By the end of the century the English fleet was almost exclusively supplied with Russian tackle. Between 1555 and 1601 four representatives of the Muscovy Company and four special royal envoys, proposed by the company, paid visits to Muscovy, some of them accompanied by a sizable entourage. It was Russian practice to enforce considerable restrictions on the freedom of movement of foreign visitors to Moscow. The English government remained cool towards Russian wishes for closer political ties.

Despite the restrictions imposed by climatic conditions English and, even more so, Dutch maritime trade with the North signified for Muscovy the opening of a window, even a door, towards the West. In addition it led to a growth in economic strength, helped the development of her northern provinces and made her particularly independent of the unsafe access routes through Poland and the Baltic

21 Riga, the great Baltic port, illustrated in a painting of *c.* 1815.

22 Arrival of a Dutch trader in Archangel. Engraving from *Historisch Verhael . . . Amsterdam*, 1677. Netherlands Embassy.

Vertreck van íyn Exelentie
COENRAET van KLENCK van ARCHANGEL

countries. In 1584 Archangel was founded. It should be noted that the Russians themselves were not complete strangers to the sea: already in the sixteenth century Russian vessels sailed to Greenland and Spitsbergen.

Western European maps from the second half of the sixteenth century (Ortelius-Jenkinson 1570, Thevet 1575) gave Europe a frontier which stretched in a south-easterly direction from the White Sea in the north to the mouth of the Don.

In the second half of the sixteenth century a number of unrealistic projects for the conquest of Muscovy were circulating in Western Europe. They originated in a mixture of sensational reports and sheer fantasy which were unverifiable at such long range, a widespread distaste for the Muscovites who were regarded as barbarians and a modern expansionist urge as experienced by European speculators and adventurers.

Two such plans for conquest came from Heinrich von Staden, a Westphalian adventurer who was in the service of Ivan IV in Moscow until 1573 or thereabouts and who had been in the *oprichniki*. But in 1578 he had entered the service of a German prince who was married to a daughter of the king of Sweden. To this man, Count Palatine Georg Hans von Veldenz-Lützelstein, a son-in-law of Gustavus Vasa, Staden outlined a plot against Muscovy which had as its objectives great commercial gains and Russian help in the struggle against the Turks. The count palatine took this plan seriously and for several years canvassed support for it among the German imperial princes and towns. About the same time Staden put an even more ambitious project before the Holy Roman Emperor Rudolf II; with the aid of ships from Spain and the Netherlands Muscovy was to be conquered by way of the White Sea and turned into a Habsburg dependency. To find such fantastic schemes among contemporary State papers is indeed strange.

More realistic were the dynastic and military projects of the *smuta* period, the Time of Troubles, which followed on the extinction of the ruling branch of the Rurik dynasty in 1598 and the death of the increasingly isolated usurper, Tsar Boris Godunov, in 1605. The Russian historian S. Platonov has said that the Time of Troubles 'moulded almost all of our history in the seventeenth century'. During this period three long-developing tendencies ended in failure: the

23 The first false Dmitri.
Woodcut made from a
brochure issued on the occasion
of his wedding by proxy in
Cracow, 1605.

attempt by the boyars, the foundations of whose power had been shattered by Ivan IV, to regain their influence by a policy of cynical opportunism; the revolt of the peasantry who under the leadership of Ivan Bolotnikov wanted the reintroduction of the right to migrate, the abolition of their economic burdens and the prevention, by social revolution, of the division of the Russian people into a ruling and a serving class, a process then in the making; the interference of neighbouring powers who wished to place foreign candidates on the throne. With the elevation to the throne of Mikhail Fedorovitch Romanov by the great Russian National Assembly of 1613, the *Zemski Sobor*, the service gentry and the merchant class emerged as the leading classes. In addition the authority of the Church, which had allied itself with those who had led the struggle against foreign invasion, was strengthened and renewed.

One such foreigner was Dmitri, allegedly the youngest son of Ivan Grozny. He came from Poland (the first Pseudodemetrius, 1605–6). The second pretender, also called Dmitri (second Pseudo-demetrius, 1608–10), although only an impostor proved to be an attractive and powerful focal point. From the north-west the Swedes intervened, from the south-west the Poles. Groups of boyars elected Vladislav, a son of the king of Poland and a member of the house of Vasa, as tsar after the conclusion of an electoral capitulation which stipulated the setting-up of a constitutional assembly. In 1610 Moscow was occupied by a Polish garrison. King Sigismund of Poland ruined the scheme by insisting that he himself should become tsar instead of his son. In 1611 a group of boyars in Novgorod declared themselves ready to elect a son of the king of Sweden as tsar. In the summer of 1612 even a Habsburg candidate appeared on the scene: Emperor Matthias proposed first a brother, then a nephew for election. But the negotiations were overtaken by the election of the native candidate Mikhail Romanov. Only the temporary paralysis of Muscovite power explains the sudden emergence and equally sudden disappearance – in 1612 – of the idea for an English protectorate in North Russia.

In risking a struggle for the possession of Livonia in 1557–58 Ivan IV rejected an alternative possibility, that of removing permanently the Tartar danger from Muscovy. The khanate of the Crimea, the only surviving remnant of the Golden Horde, was to remain a lasting threat, all the more so from 1475 when it came under Turkish suzerainty. From then on it was regarded as an outpost of the Ottoman Empire. The Turkish fortress of Azov closed the mouth of the Don while the khan of the Crimea burned down Moscow in 1571 and renewed the tsar's obligation to pay tribute.

Warding off the Tartars was a matter of such moment in the first half of the seventeenth century that Muscovy sought to protect her southern border by the erection of an elaborately fortified *limes* dotted with defensive works and settlements. This defensive line with its more than thirty towns and numerous observation posts fitted in with European assumptions concerning Russia's later policy towards Turkey. But at this time the Black Sea or even more distant conquests were still far beyond Muscovy's dreams.

The mid-seventeenth century saw a change in Moscow's relations with other states; for the incorporation of the Ukraine, the ancient territory of Kiev, brought with it Muscovite involvement in Polish–Turkish disputes. In Kiev, which had come under Lithuanian rule in the fourteenth century and together with Great Lithuania had later come under the influence and sovereignty of Poland, a new self-awareness developed in the Greek Orthodox Church in the 1630s and 1640s under the influence of Metropolitan Peter Mohyla (Mogila). This was a response to the attempt being made by active Catholics, particularly Polish Jesuits, to reunite the churches and it took the form of latinizing the thought and language of the Church, in agreement, liturgically and dogmatically, with the Greek Church of the Balkan peninsula. Because Russian liturgy had diverged from the Greek norm differences arose between Moscow and Kiev which could only be resolved by a reform of the Muscovite Church.

The Kievan Church's strongest support was the frontier republic which had been developed on the Lower Dnieper by the free Cossacks, the *Zaporozhye*. This defence force was so strong that it was able to make agreements with its neighbours, the Crimean Tartars, the Porte and its co-religionist the Muscovite tsar and to play off one against another. But it was not strong enough to maintain itself independently of them. When the Cossacks placed themselves under the 'ruling hand' of the Muscovite tsar in 1654 in order to hold on to their political autonomy it brought about war with Poland. After a number of indecisive battles and months of diplomatic wrangling the Russians gained new political and territorial advantages in the Treaty of Andrussovo in 1667, bringing under Muscovite rule that part of the Ukraine on the left bank of the Dnieper, Smolensk and – for a two-year period – Kiev.

In the hope of winning back what she had lost Poland allied herself with the Turks, who were now pushing forward in a new wave of expansion. The first military clash between the Turks, backed by the khanate of the Crimea, and the Russo-Ukrainian army took place in the Ukraine in 1677, and it was won by the latter. Although the twenty-year truce concluded at Bakhtchiserai in the Crimea in 1681 left Muscovy in possession of the left bank of the Dnieper it did not release the tsars from the payment of tribute.

From 1672 Moscow came to realize the necessity of an alliance of all the Christian powers against the Turkish threat. When King John Sobieski of Poland with the help of the army of the Holy Roman Empire defeated the Turks on the Kahlenberg near Vienna in 1683 prayers of thanksgiving were offered in the churches of Moscow. In 1684 imperial envoys, supported by a papal delegate, were in Moscow negotiating the accession of Muscovy to the Holy League, the offensive alliance against the Infidel, which had been formed by the emperor, the king of Poland and the Venetian Republic under papal patronage. Moscow made its accession to the alliance conditional on a final settlement with Poland on the basis of the Andrussovo treaty. Thus the Eternal Peace with Poland was concluded in the spring of 1686. It laid the foundations for an offensive alliance against the Turks and Tartars and established a connection with the Holy League. Muscovy pledged itself to enter the war against the Turks in the

24, 25 Medals struck to commemorate the Treaty of Eternal Peace, 1686, between Moscow and Poland: (left) King John Sobieski, (right) personification of Poland and Russia. Hermitage, Leningrad.

following year, justifying the breach of the truce by asserting that the Turks and Tartars had disturbed the peace.

Muscovy's *rapprochement* with Poland was successful because of the common danger from the Turks, but the tsars were not so fortunate in their relations with Sweden. Since Gustavus II Adolphus had blocked Muscovy completely from access to the Baltic in the Peace of Stolbovo in 1617, the reconquest at least of the Greek Orthodox territories on the Gulf of Finland, which had once belonged to Novgorod, as well as Ingermanland and eastern Karelia remained an unaccomplished goal. During Sweden's incursion into great power politics in the seventeenth century Muscovy remained for a long time her ally. Sweden was the first European power to establish a permanent embassy at the court of the tsar. During the Thirty Years War Muscovy supported Sweden by supplying her with wheat, and included as an ally of Sweden in the Peace of Westphalia (Osnabrück 1648) was the *magnus dux Muscoviae*.

By the foundation of Nyen on the Neva in 1632 the Swedes were the first to see and develop the commercial and political potential of what was Russia's shortest water route to the Baltic. The war which Russia waged against Sweden between 1656 and 1661 immediately brought military victories on the Neva and in Livonia – among others the conquest of Nyen and the reoccupation of Dorpat in 1656 – but it also brought defeats such as the unsuccessful siege of Riga. And finally Muscovy had to retreat. The Peace of Kardis (summer 1661) confirmed the frontiers agreed on at Stolbovo. Tartar and Turkish pressure in the south prevented the Muscovite government from renewing the war against Sweden, although Denmark and Brandenburg offered themselves as allies. In 1684 the peace was confirmed.

One can sum up by saying that in the sixteenth century the old European world finding itself threatened in far-distant Livonia, a territory allied to the Holy Roman Empire but early influenced by the Reformation, saw the Russian aggressor as an alien, hostile to Europe. In the seventeenth century continental Europe recognized the Christian Russians as co-fighters in the defensive war against the Turks. That Russia had two faces, one alien, one familiar, that she could be a powerful and menacing enemy as well as a highly valued friend was an experience which has since then sunk into the innermost recesses of Western consciousness.

The rush to admit West European experts, to accept foreign customs, to introduce new techniques and to make use of new tools grew stronger in Muscovy from one decade to the next but, generally speaking, only in the capital. Although foreigners from a number of nations – officers, doctors, merchants, translators among others – were forced to live in an isolated suburb near Moscow, the *nemetskaya sloboda*, their isolation cannot have been complete. From the 1660s a regular letter, money and parcel post to the West was in existence. The Church, supported by the tsar, wanted to preserve the traditional way of life, and resisted the introduction of external influences: the foreign clothes and wig of one of the tsar's relatives were burned in 1653 on the patriarch's order, and even in 1675 both Church and tsar reacted against the shaving of beards with prohibitions and threats of punishment. Tobacco, prohibited by both Church and State as a drug, was smuggled in and widely used.

Because of Russia's resistance to foreign influence there was a tendency to label the introduction of reforms as 'Europeanization'. But this missed the point. It must not be forgotten that Russian craft production – often without foreign stimulation – went through a process of specialization, differentiation and refinement. The concentration of the Russian home market, with Moscow becoming by far its strongest centre, was a completely independent occurrence while the extension of its Asian trade was achieved by Russian traders with State support. Chinese porcelain, imported into Europe by sea, was brought to Moscow by the overland route in the seventeenth century. In many respects the Ukraine, from the time of its union with

Muscovy, was the intermediary for modern intellectual trends. Many Western influences – despite the hereditary enmity – arrived in Russia through Poland. Many European expressions common in the technical world, and in the areas of natural science and political institutions were absorbed via Polish, e.g. *apteka, kantselyariya, politika, muzyka*. The co-existence of men of fundamentally different stamp among the Muscovite aristocracy at the end of the seventeenth century is striking, varying from old-fashioned patriarchal types to modern-minded figures. Among those prominent as pro-Europeans was Prince Vassily Vassilevich Golitsyn, favourite of the Regent Sophia, who as head of the department of foreign affairs concluded both the peace with Poland in 1686 and the alliance with the Catholic powers.

But the West also had two faces: the cult of pious traditions, intellectual strength and the force of the Counter-Reformation on one side, on the other the refugees, the polemics, doubt and the rationalism as serious as it was ironical. During the last years of the seventeenth century the boyar Boris Petrovich Sheremetev travelled to Italy and Malta. This man, later one of Peter the Great's generals, saw only an old-fashioned ecclesiastical world: in Rome he visited one church after another, went from one monastery to the next and received with tears in his eyes a miraculous cross from the hands of the pope. In Naples he saw how the wonder-working blood of John the Baptist, kept in a nunnery, liquefied and rose mysteriously and alarmingly in its receptacle. In Malta this boyar was entertained by the Knights of St John.

Russia was already changing rapidly when Tsar Peter, born in 1672, was pushed forward by his relatives and followers into taking over control of the State from his half-sister, the Regent Sophia (1689). The seventeen-year-old boy was not the first Russian to look for acquaintances in the German suburb, but he was the first Russian tsar to do so. As yet his toy soldiers and his sailing boats did not herald revolution.

As already mentioned Muscovy was again at war with Turkey in 1687. The two campaigns, which Prince Golitsyn waged in the Crimea in 1687 and 1689, failed but they removed the pressure from the allies of the Holy Roman Emperor. When Peter decided on military activity the direction it took – against the Crescent – was predestined for him. His first campaign, too, was a failure. But his second achieved its objective, the conquest of Azov.

26 Detail of icon painting, *Virgin of Vladimir*, by
S. Ushakov, 1668, showing Tsar Alexis (1645–76)
and the Spassky Gate at the Moscow Kremlin.

27 Medal struck on the occasion of the birth of Peter the Great in 1672, who became tsar at the age of nine, with his half-sister Sophia as regent. Museum of History and Reconstruction, Moscow.

28 Execution of the Streltzy in 1699; these were soldiers of the Moscow garrison who rose against Peter I when he was abroad. Engraving from *Diarium Itineris in Moscoviam* by Joannes Georgius Korb, 1700. British Museum.

When in the spring of 1696 the tsar besieged the Turkish fortress at the mouth of the Don, Santa Croce, the papal nuncio in Poland, wrote to Cardinal Spada, the papal secretary of state, saying that nobody could be more favourably disposed towards the Holy League than Tsar Peter. After the fall of Azov in July 1696 while Peter was preparing the Great Embassy to Western Europe he sent two-thirds of the young aristocrats destined for naval training away to Italy, and the remaining third to the United Provinces. The Embassy, which the tsar himself wished to accompany under a pseudonym, was to travel to Rome and Venice, via Vienna, thence to Holland and England and finally to Brandenburg. But *en route* the itinerary was changed and the United Provinces became its first destination.

This great journey brought a tsar – half incognito – to Western Europe for the first time; to Germany, Holland and England. The trip failed in its primary purpose, the strengthening of the Christian front against the Turks. The States-General refused to deliver the ships which the tsar sought; the king of England, William of Orange, paved the way for peace negotiations between the emperor and the Porte behind the backs of the Russians, and Vienna, anyway, was determined to make peace because of the dispute over the Spanish Succession. No longer were there anywhere grounds for a crusade. The visit to Venice, where Peter was already expected, had to be abandoned when internal unrest in Russia recalled the tsar to Moscow.

In every other respect the visit, which lasted altogether one and a half years, was successful and, from the historical point of view, exceptionally important. In the United Provinces the Russians were able to observe the Ryswick negotiations at close quarters and to make

contact with half the diplomats of Europe. The network of power-interests was instructive, especially as it was totally alien to the Eastern pattern. On different occasions the tsar met famous contemporaries, William of Orange, whom he had admired from childhood, in Utrecht and in London, and in Vienna Prince Eugene of Savoy, although nothing is definitely known about this meeting. Leibniz did not approach the delegation; his meeting with the tsar belongs to a later period. From Holland Peter brought back much information, many ideas and lasting impressions. It touched almost the whole European horizon when Russia adopted the St Andrew's cross with its Maltese tradition as the flag of the navy. The colours white-blue-red were borrowed from the United Provinces for the merchant marine flag which later became the Russian national flag. So both the old and the new Europe were symbolized in the two flags of the empire.

Peter gained his most important impressions in England. There he was able to satisfy his desire to understand the theory of shipbuilding, having already acquired practical expertise in the Netherlands. He had the opportunity to take part in a fleet manœuvre out of Portsmouth. Whether or not the tsar met Newton, who that year became master of the Royal Mint, is not known. Bishop Gilbert Burnet with whom the tsar held long theological discussions – as mentioned earlier – said in a letter written at that time how impressed he was with the tsar's knowledge. But for Peter many things in England remained a closed book: the position of Parliament was incomprehensible to him and he saw the curtailment of royal power as an infringment of the royal dignity. But the Russian school of navigation which he established was formed on the English pattern with English teachers. Perhaps the

49

core of Peter's social reforms, the Succession Law of 1714, derived from English precedents. Peter picked up endless new ideas in the Netherlands as well as in England, at the German courts and at Vienna. For his intended reforms he recruited about a thousand specialists.

Among the plethora of equipment, activities and skills the tsar was most attracted by everything that offered sustenance to his craving for knowledge and that promised to increase his power; the connection between natural laws and mechanics, the rapid, intelligent, practical application of newly discovered principles across the whole sweep of life. Thus he adapted to his own purpose the strongest impulses of the early Enlightenment. In time he became aware of the leverage which scientific knowledge gave him. Man, so it might seem to him, could only reach his goal by seizing on technology: a future, still opaque but with immeasurable outlines stretched before him, a future of tremendous appeal – the whole of modern times.

The refusal of the European powers to continue their joint military action against the Turks, absorbed as they were in their own affairs, gave the tsar the opportunity to attack Sweden with the help of the kings of Denmark and Poland in the autumn of 1700. The coalition, which in 1719–20 under the leadership of British diplomacy sought to hinder the victorious tsar from acquiring the Baltic lands, was incapable of action because of conflicting individual interests. The *raison d'état* of nation-state aims, the transmission of technical skills, the expansive spirit of the times, all served, directly or indirectly, to incorporate Russia in the world of the European state system.

Of the twenty-six and a half years which remained to him after his great journey to the West the tsar spent twenty-one of them waging war for possession of the Baltic coast. After his triumphant victory over Charles XII at Poltava (1709) and the conquest of Estonia and Livonia (1710) he continued the war from northern Germany (1711–17); then, with support from Prussia and Hanover, unhindered by the British fleet, embarked on the direct invasion of Sweden itself. Turkey's entry into the war, brought about by Charles XII, was but an interlude. Because of the disadvantages of his position Peter was ready to settle for the retention of St Petersburg, founded by him in 1703 on the Neva. In 1710 the nobility of Livonia and Estonia and the towns of Riga and Reval paid homage to him. The Treaty of Nystad (1721) confirmed his possession of them and left the new provinces their ancient representative institutions.

From then on Russia had a new face. In 1712 Tsar Peter decreed that Russians were no longer to be called 'Muscovites'. The new capital on the Neva with its Dutch-German name, its façade of stone palaces, its many foreigners, its dockyards and workshops and its pretensions to maritime trade symbolized the tsar's renunciation of Moscow and many of its traditions. St Petersburg, however, became a Russian city, certainly one facing the modern age. The Baltic provinces of Livonia and Estonia, in which everything was very different from what it was in Russia – the people and their institutions, the law and the Church – provided their new sovereign with many Germans for the service of the State and they welcomed foreign visitors to Russia in German, and in un-Russian towns. The introduction of the title of 'emperor' into these provinces by Peter in 1710, long before he took the title officially (1721) had a deep significance: this title of 'emperor' was a modern one, not something taken over from Byzantine tradition; nor was it to be seen as a synonym for 'czar', but as a replacement for it. 'The establishment of this empire', Voltaire wrote later, 'is perhaps Europe's greatest event, after the discovery of the New World.' The modern historian will agree with this, with some slight reservations.

Of course the victorious conclusion of the Great Northern War brought about a shift in the balance of power: henceforth Russia, not Sweden, was the dominant power in the North. The military superiority of a modernized and activated Russian Empire forced both the small duchy of Courland and the formerly powerful Polish State into dependency. So much had Russia changed that in 1721 an informative account of the country could be published in Frankfurt under the title *Das veränderte Russland*. A strong fleet was created from nothing, its jargon borrowed from English and Dutch; the enlarged regular army was provided with German ranks and its fire-power was strengthened. Technical schools were founded; to the thirteen factories already existing 178 new ones were added, some of them very large ones. New departments of state were founded on foreign models, their administrative units labelled in the language of the foreign original. The income of the State was increased. The Patriarchate was allowed to lapse and the administration of the Church taken over by the State. There were numerous other reforms.

But it must be made clear that a number of these reforms had begun before Peter's reign: the fundamental reforms in the field of industrial

29 Peter I was determined to make his country a naval power. This contemporary engraving shows part of his fleet. *Diarium Itineris in Moscoviam* by J. G. Korb, 1700. British Museum.

production, the expansion of trade, the modernization of the army, the emancipation from clerical influence, the immigration of foreigners; but the development of these reforms was speeded up – and complicated – by the restless genius of the tsar. Before Peter the Great's time Russia was already a power with whom her neighbours had to reckon, whom they feared or sought to use. While it is true that Peter institutionalized and strengthened Russia's great-power status, recognition of his title of emperor was refused him by the Holy Roman Empire, Britain, France, Spain and Poland. The attempt to assimilate Western European practices into Russia's social conditions and way of life was only partly successful; the general school policy was a failure, representative local government – partly an imitation of the pattern obtaining in the Baltic provinces – struck no roots, the division of the population into two classes, a privileged class and a tax-paying class, was accentuated. Above all the great reformer's peasant policy was a fiasco: serfdom was intensified and the peasantry levelled into one uniform mass.

Not to understand the contrast between the intention and the reality of the new Russia as an inducement towards the continuation and strengthening of the reform policy is to be in danger of accepting appearances in lieu of reality. The Russian ruling class did not escape this danger in the eighteenth century – or later.

30 Peter the Great holding the infant Louis XV in his arms, 1717, at the Hôtel de Lesdiguières in Paris. Painting by Mme L. M. J. Hersent (1784–1862). Musée de Versailles.

In the great emperor's relationship with the West two attitudes predominated: on the one hand a willingness to learn and an assimilation of all that was useful (even during his visit to Paris in 1717 the tsar absorbed many new ideas); on the other hand there was a consciousness of independence, of his own power, even a sense of superiority. His actions were on a vast scale but he was certainly not what the nineteenth-century forgery, passing as his Testament, stated: the emperor who through continuous warfare strove for the expansion of Russia in all directions. After Sweden's defeat the new empire took her place among the great powers, participating like other states in the classical balance of power policy.

Uncertainty regarding the succession was one of the problems bequeathed to his heirs by Peter the Great: his eldest son Alexei, whom he feared would destroy his work, was tortured to death in 1718 after being accused of treason; two other sons died in infancy; one of the two daughters born to him before his marriage was engaged to Duke Karl Friedrich of Holstein. By the time of his death Peter had not named his successor, a right reserved to the autocrat by the Succession Law of 1722. As a result one usurpation followed another: firstly Peter's widow Catherine, a former Lithuanian servant-girl who had been his mistress for years before he married her, then Peter II, his

31 Empress Elizabeth in
riding habit.
Painting by George
Christoph Groot,
1743. Tretyakov
Gallery, Moscow.

eleven-year-old grandson from Alexei's marriage to a princess of Brunswick-Wolfenbüttel, with whose death in 1730 the male line of the Romanovs ceased. His successor was Peter's niece, Anna Ivanovna, widow of the duke of Courland and sister of the duchess of Mecklenburg. She allowed herself to be dominated by her lover, the Courlander Biron whom she created duke of Courland. After a Mecklenburg interlude Peter's illegitimate daughter Elizabeth ascended the throne by a *coup d'état* in 1740. She named her nephew by the Holstein marriage of her sister as her heir. This grandson of Peter the Great, the feeble-minded Emperor Peter III, was murdered in the summer of 1762, leaving the dynasty the name of Holstein-Gottorp. His widow, a German-born princess, became Catherine II.

Had the dynasty become Europeanized? An examination of the advisers, courtiers and higher officials does reinforce that impression. It is true that many Russians who had served under Peter the Great remained in positions of influence but the attempt of the Russian higher nobility to restrict the power of the Empress Anna quickly failed. In Russian historical literature the reign of Anna bears the label *Bironovshchina*, and even carries the stigma of being a period of German rule. This is misleading as the 'Germans' did not form a closed group during these years. Count Münnich, a hydraulics engineer from Oldenburg, who planned the Ladoga canal and

32 Peter the Great. Painting by Louis Karavack. Hermitage, Leningrad.

became a Russian field marshal, ousted Biron in 1740. But he was himself toppled in 1741 by Baron Ostermann, the son and grandson of Westphalian pastors who was married to a Russian lady related to the imperial house. For half a generation – until his own downfall in 1741 – Ostermann had conducted Russian foreign policy in the spirit of Peter the Great's adroit power politics.

It is true that almost every single thing which in Russia was seen as evidence of foreign influence dated back to Peter the Great's 'Europeanization' programme, the four marriage alliances which he arranged with German princely houses and the employment of foreign technicians. But Peter's inheritance shows the futility of moralizing about 'Europeanization' or even drawing an analogy between it and a specifically 'Russian' way. Russia had to play her part in the concert of the powers, using the weapons of the period, according to the conventions of the period. The question of a diminution of Russia's power potential does not arise.

In 1734 the first specific trade agreement, not a political alliance, made by a Russian Government was concluded with Britain. By this Britain bought at least two-thirds of Russia's most important exports (hemp, flax, linen, iron). In form drawn up in accordance with the principle of equality the treaty gave all the advantages to the British, who were able to extend considerably their economic ascendancy in Russia (D. Gerhard). To the Russians the increase in exports was so important as to outweigh all other considerations. The political alliance with Britain which followed in 1742 corresponded with Russia's Habsburg-oriented foreign policy and her enmity to France, which was itself conditioned by her relationship with Poland and Turkey.

In Poland Russia favoured the Saxon candidate for the throne against the French-supported Polish king. During the Turkish War (1735–39) it was Münnich – not a Russian – who put before Empress Anna the conquest of Constantinople as an imperial aim, though at the time this objective was both politically and militarily beyond her reach.

Russia's difficulty in catching up with the West in the scientific field is shown by the history of two great institutions which first came into being under Peter the Great's successors. These were the Imperial Academy of Sciences at St Petersburg, founded by Peter the Great but opened after his death in 1725, and Russia's first university, founded in Moscow (1755) in the reign of his daughter Elizabeth by Ivan Ivanovich Shuvalov. At first both the academy and the university were heavily dependent on foreign scholars. Of the 111 members of the St Petersburg Academy in the eighteenth century 68 were men whose mother-tongue was German, 26 were Russians and the rest came from various other nations (E. Amburger). In the long view these 'symbols of higher education' (Stökl) played a most important role in controlling the training and advancement of Russia's own scientific establishment. To this belonged that universal genius Mikhail Lomonosov who acquired the foundations of his scientific education at Marburg. Even before participating in the foundation of Moscow University Lomonosov demonstrated in the Academy of Sciences a novel nationalistic self-assertiveness, no longer 'old Muscovite' in tone but modern European: in an address in 1749 he condemned the theory that the Russian State originated with the Normans.

In 1711 Russian troops made their first appearance in Western Europe, in Pomerania, Holstein and Mecklenburg, coming not as conquerors but as part of Peter the Great's strategy during the Great Northern War. During the War of the Polish Succession a small Russian army appeared in Germany for the second time, marching through Silesia, Bohemia and Franconia to the Rhine. The third occasion on which Russian troops fought on German soil was during the Seven Years War. Defeated by Frederick the Great at Zorndorf in 1758, the Russians together with their Austrian allies were victorious at Kunersdorf. In October 1760 they occupied Berlin, while from 1757 they held East Prussia.

Under the impression that war would waken the Russians from their lethargy and that it was Russia's mission to dictate the law of action to the other powers the Russian chancellor, A. P. Bestuzhev-Ryumin deliberately engineered Russia's entrance into the war in 1756. In fact Russia's participation in the military and political decisions of this war, for those classes touched by it, was the beginning of a new vitality and self-confidence. A foreign adventurer (d'Eon), having come into possession of information in St Petersburg – probably in the years 1755–60 – drew up a memorandum which served as the basis for the so-called Testament of Peter the Great – as if Peter would have recommended his successors to engage in continuous wars of conquest.

East Prussia, at first nothing more than a bargaining-counter became in time a war objective: in the Austro-Russian convention of 1 April 1760 Russia secured for herself the permanent cession of the province – the so-called kingdom of Prussia – in the event of Austria winning back Silesia and Glatz. But the death of Elizabeth and Peter III's accession presaged a change in policy. The new emperor, an admirer of Frederick the Great, immediately concluded a truce with Prussia, renouncing in the peace treaty of May 1762 all conquests and compensations and evacuating East Prussia.

During the four and a half years of the Russian occupation the inhabitants of East Prussia experienced two different facets of Russian rule. Stationed among them, in addition to fifty regiments of regular troops, were 14,000 Cossacks, 2,000 Tartars and 1,000 Kalmuks. That the irregular troops were guilty of atrocities is not denied in the memoirs of A. T. Bolotov, a Russian officer who served as interpreter and aide-de-camp to the Russian governor-general of the conquered province, but there was probably much exaggeration. Excesses were severely punished by the commander-in-chief, Fermor, a Russian-born Scot settled in Livonia. But fear of the Russians was awakened by the call of Field Marshal Apraksin, the first commander-in-chief, that all inhabitants of standing and all professional people should emigrate to Russia. On the other hand there is no denying that all classes and authorities in the province took an oath of allegiance to the Empress Elizabeth as their new sovereign in 1757–58. Numerous high officers in the Russian forces were non-Russian in origin, most of them being Germans from the Baltic provinces. The Russian governor-general, residing in the Prussian coronation city of Königsberg, was the German-speaking Courlander J. N. von Korff. He was unable to write Russian, although married to a Russian, and his personal staff consisted mainly of German-speaking officials and clerks. In Königsberg Korff kept open house and gave balls which were attended by the German aristocracy of the province. In much the same way Russian officers thronged the palace of Graf J. G. von Keyserling. The openhearted, outgoing manner of the Russian authorities was, however, politically motivated; for it was designed to win over the province's governing class. The University of Königsberg was especially favoured and Russian army officers even attended the lectures of Immanuel Kant. There is ample evidence that the easy-living style of the Russians loosened up Königsberg's narrow provincial exclusiveness and helped to lower the class barriers. At the same time, Königsberg's incorporation into those society circles that wielded influence in Mitau, Riga and St Petersburg helped to 'aristocratize' the city (K. Stavenhagen).

Certainly the Russian ruling class, especially court society in St Petersburg, was by no means homogeneous in the eighteenth century. As at Versailles and those other courts which aped it the position of the peasants grew steadily worse and the court and the court nobility displayed their luxurious way of life at the expense of the dependent and serving classes. In Peter the Great's system the nobleman was under obligation to serve the State, but after the death of the great autocrat he was able to evade this consequence of his privileged status more and more. Empress Anna reduced his obligations, while Peter III abolished almost all of them. The manifesto of 18 February 1762 'On the Granting of Freedom to the Well-born Russian Aristocracy' was based on the theory that obligatory service had been necessary in the past so as to inculcate the spirit of patriotism, but that that was no longer necessary. However it was hoped that the nobility would not withdraw from service, and hostility to service and to education were regarded with general contempt. An important point was freedom of movement; journeys abroad as well as service in foreign states by such aristocrats as were not already in service at home was no longer subject to licence. Almost the only obligation retained by the aristocracy was that of immediate return from abroad when ordered by the government. The eighteenth-century Russian aristocrat experienced an effective alienation from the State (M. Raeff).

In time more and more differences among the aristocracy revealed themselves. Many nobles, educated by foreign tutors, were barely able to express themselves in Russian while the great mass of land-owners, living on their estates, understood no other language. Ivan Shuvalov, the founder of Moscow University, turned against the strong influence wielded by those who spoke foreign languages, demanding that in the guards, the army and the navy three-quarters of the generals must be Russian, the other quarter to be made up of Livonians, Estonians and foreigners. But it was extremely difficult to enforce such decrees. Russians of all classes had first to develop the skills and abilities necessary for the proper functioning of all the new posts created by this vast empire. The road from Moscow to St Petersburg was long.

III EUROPEAN HEGEMONY

'Russia is a European power' (*Rossiya yest' yevropeyskaya derzhava*). In this succint style Catherine II announced in 1766, in a hand-written outline to the famous Instruction, the *Nakaz*, her programme for the Legislative Commission which she was to set up. In a letter to Frederick the Great she described, with a touch of self-irony, how she had acted like the raven in the fable, which adorned itself with the feathers of the peacock. In the same vein she informed d'Alembert in 1765 that he would see 'how I have ransacked President de Montes-quieu without acknowledgment, for the benefit of my empire'. And she hoped that when Montesquieu, watching her from beyond the grave, saw her working, 'he will forgive this plagiarism, for the good of twenty million people'. In her spirited way she let it be understood that in the composition of her principles of government she was inspired by the ideas of the Enlightenment.

Catherine, the daughter of a Prussian general, had been married in 1745 to her cousin Peter of Holstein-Gottorp, grandson of Peter the Great and heir to the Russian throne. Having brought about the deposition of her husband and acquiesced in his assassination she ascended the throne in 1762, with the assistance of officers of the guards. This usurper, dependent on the support of the aristocracy in domestic affairs, perfectly understood how to make Russia forget her foreign origin and how to coax Europe into crediting her with a reputation for enlightenment. During her years as grand duchess she had familiarized herself with the political and philosophical literature of the Enlightenment. She had read, among others, Montesquieu and Bayle, Grotius and Beccaria, Voltaire, Diderot and d'Alembert and she carried on a correspondence with various moulders of public opinion in Western Europe, particularly with Voltaire and the Encyclopedists.

The empress's letters, elegant and light, occasionally even frivolous, were a most skilfully primed source of information and political propaganda. She kept 'l'illustre hermite de Ferney' informed about her plans and her successes, casually introducing into her letters

< 33 Catherine II, the Great. Painting by Vigilius Erichsen (1722–82). Kensington Palace. Probably presented to George III. Reproduced by gracious permission of Her Majesty the Queen.

laudatory snippets about Russia; the people, the language, the country. From Moscow in March 1767 she praised 'the richness and conciseness of our language', which made it so difficult to translate. 'My soldiers', she boasted in 1769, 'go to war against the Turks as they would to a wedding.' Russia alone, among all the nations of Europe, would gain the laurels in this war against the barbarians. 'Our nation', she wrote, 'has, in general, the happiest disposition in the world: there is nothing easier than to give them a taste for goodness and reasonableness' (1770). Catherine liked to hint to her French correspondents at the vastness and complexity of her empire. She recommended Riga – the former Hansa town with its German magistracy and its predominantly German population – as being 'as good as Leipzig' for the study of German. From Kazan she wrote in 1767: 'here I am in Asia', in a town in which people from twenty different races lived; to find for all her peoples an appropriate polity 'is almost to create a world, to unite it, to conserve it, etc.' In her embroidered reports on Russian social conditions the empress went so far as to claim that the Russian peasant had not only a 'chicken in his pot' but that some of the peasants 'preferred turkey'. In diplomatic affairs Catherine also set out to influence public opinion in the West. On occasion Voltaire lent her his support; he had been persuaded to back Catherine's *coup d'état* in a report which had been personally approved by her. And at a later date he was to give public approval to her Polish policy.

The Legislative Commission, which Catherine II set up with such a modern flair for publicity – she had copies of the Instruction distributed abroad in Latin, French and German – met in Moscow in August 1767. As most of its members had been elected it was almost a representative assembly. In a well planned distribution of seats the townspeople, mainly merchants, with 207 seats composed the strongest group among the 564 representatives, followed by the aristocracy with 165 seats, the free State peasants with 78, then the Cossacks and a great number of national minorities (Bashkirs, Tartars, Samoyeds, etc.). This mixed assembly, which discussed various economic and social issues and passed on to the government valuable information along with some 1,500 written instructions from the electorates, encompassed the whole ethnical, religious, cultural and sociological sweep of the empire. Sitting beside exotic Mohammedans from the East were German Lutherans from Estonia and Livonia, not all of whom could speak Russian but who were often learned men. Alongside highly educated Russian aristocrats sat numerous illiterates. But the serfs, by far the most numerous class in the population, were not represented. Western observers quickly recognized that the pretentious abstractions of the imperial Instruction – fame and freedom, bourgeois society, equality before the law – bore no relation to Russian social reality. From the British Embassy in St Petersburg the secretary, Henry Shirley, reported on 10 March 1768, not without a hint of mockery, on the provincial deputies in the Commission: 'To give Your Lordship a right idea of this choice collection of men, and their operations, permit me to suppose a certain number of the most ignorant of our petty merchants and shopkeepers in Great Britain and Ireland gathered as the several deputies of those nations in America, who either are subjects, or under the protection of His Majesty, and a few gentlemen unacquainted with the general principles, which constitute the basis of good government; this would be perhaps too favourable a copy of the original, now in possession of what Russia prides herself so much upon.'

This Moscow Assembly cannot be compared with the English Parliament, the *Etats Généraux* in France or even with the Swedish *Riksdag*. Catherine, of course, provoked such comparisons by giving her scheme a theoretical framework derived from Western European political traditions. It cannot have been her intention to set up a permanent representative assembly. It is even doubtful if she really intended the Commission to produce a new code of law, the aim which she had set before it. The open discussions were, in themselves, of value for the government but the Commission's only decision, embedded in much formality and publicized in the newspapers in Russian, German and French, concerned the dignity of the empress. On the proposal of the highest authorities, the Senate and the Synod, the Assembly decided on 9 August 1767 to confer on the empress the titles 'Catherine the Great' and 'Most Wise Mother of the Fatherland'. This was a very elaborate imitation of the proceedings in 1721 when the Roman-sounding title of 'Father of the Fatherland' and 'The Great' were bestowed on Peter I at the same time as he was proclaimed emperor. But that was based on the reality of Peter's achievements. Now it was but an empty gesture, its political purpose quite obviously the legitimization of the usurper through comparison with her great predecessor, so as to make her position unassailable. The Commission,

63

transferred to St Petersburg, was dissolved on the outbreak of the Turkish War.

What Catherine strove for in her domestic policy was a centralized authority underpinned by the aristocracy. The loss of its autonomous status by the Ukraine in 1764 and the Cossack constitution of 1775 served this purpose. In the Legislative Commission a unity of interests bound together the Ukrainian deputies and the representatives from Estonia and Livonia. Catherine wished the Commission to speak out against the special legal position of the Baltic provinces and Russian deputies complied with her desires. But in spite of this she did not abolish their privileges.

As far as local government was concerned Catherine's policy was as riddled with contradictions as that of her great predecessor. Peter the Great as well as Catherine wanted active and unprompted co-operation from the upper classes but without any encroachment on their autocracy. The difference in attitude between the two rulers was, of course, that Peter the Great insisted on the obligation of the aristocracy to serve the State while Catherine supported their exemption from service. It is a baffling paradox that the enlightened empress who had planned to reform the legal position of the peasantry should have contributed more to the deprivation of their rights than any of her predecessors. Indicative of this was the depression of the private peasant's status caused by her presentation of about 400,000 State peasants to her favourites and lovers. Certainly behind the empress's peasant policy were the enormous material interests of the landowning aristocracy, to which she trimmed her measures. But this, of course, must not be seen in too mechanical a way: part of the problem was the fateful weakness of the empress herself. It was a threefold weakness; as a foreigner as well as an usurper she needed the backing of the strongest social class while the inveterate nymphomaniac treated State interests as a reserve currency in her sexual adventures, coupling the game of *libido voluptatum* with that of *libido dominandi* though from her accession only Russians were chosen as official favourites. In her person Catherine represented an extreme variation of the problem 'Russia' or 'Europe'. She, the most Western-oriented of Russian rulers, in some ways furthered most Russia's alienation from the West.

The most effective of Catherine's administrative reforms was not the measure for the improvement of local government through corporate representation but the strengthening of regional government through the extension of the role of the *gouverneur*, described as the 'head and master of the *gouvernement*'. In individual cases such a position might have been the means of introducing Western ideas and institutions into Russia. As *gouverneur* of one of the largest of Russian *gouvernements* – Novgorod – Catherine II appointed in 1764 Jakob Johann von Sievers, a thirty-three-year-old retired major-general and a member of the German nobility in Livonia, whose formative years had been spent in England. Working in close co-operation with the empress Sievers reformed the province by persuading the aristocracy to accept social responsibility, by insisting on protection for the serfs, by modernizing agriculture, cutting canals, etc. Catherine also sought his opinion on legal reform but without allowing him a central role. It was on his advice that the empress issued her secret decree abolishing torture in 1767, as it was on his recommendation that Charlotte von Lieven, an exceptionally able and distinguished woman, was appointed governess of Catherine's grandchildren – afterwards the emperors Alexander I and Nicholas I. She was created a countess by Paul I and a princess by Nicholas I. Sievers himself retired in 1782, no longer able to prevail against the empress's powerful favourites, and he had to wait until Paul's accession to be created a count.

Although Russia's assimilation of the modes of the European Enlightenment – highly exaggerated by the empress and her propagandists – was in reality incomplete, fragmentary and superficial yet Russia's own impact on the European state system was immense.

From the time of Peter the Great Poland was susceptible to Russian pressure and influence. How much this was taken for granted at St Petersburg is shown in Catherine II's attitude to the young Pole Stanislav August Poniatovski. Writing to him in August 1762 – just a month after her usurpation of power – she informed him that she was sending an envoy to Poland immediately 'to make you king'. Poniatovski (to whom – as it has been gallantly said – Catherine, while still grand duchess, 'had not refused any favours') was related to the so-called 'family', the Czartoryski party, which looked to Russia for support in its plans for Poland's reconstruction. The Russian envoy at Warsaw – together with Prince Repnin – was the Courlander Count Keyserling who already in August 1762 proposed to the Prussian envoy in St Petersburg closer co-operation on Polish issues.

34 Solemn fête at St Petersburg, arranged by Alexander I on 12 May 1803, centenary of its foundation by Peter the Great. Coloured lithograph by Gabriel Lory, 1804. Gottfried-Keller-Stiftung, Zürich.

In April 1764 a Russo-Prussian treaty was signed which included a reciprocal guarantee of the territories of both powers and mutual assurances of support. And in a secret article the two powers agreed on a common Polish policy. Both powers showed an interest in the situation of Polish dissenters. A long-standing excuse for Russian interference in Polish affairs was Russia's concern that Poland's Greek Orthodox minority should have equal rights with the Catholic majority. From this time onwards Russo-Prussian understanding was largely at Poland's expense. Prussia, burdened by her doubtful right to Silesia, depended on Russia's support, while the Prussian alliance was for Russia an excellent cover for the establishment of her domination over Poland.

The First Partition of Poland was based on Prusso-Russian co-operation, as was Poniatovski's election as king in 1764, but Russia was, by far, the senior partner. Although Frederick the Great had no illusions as far as the growth of Russian power was concerned, he renewed his alliance with Russia in 1769. The agreement between the two powers on the appropriation of large areas of Poland – the First Partition – was not in conformity with Catherine's ultimate goal; for she would have preferred indirect control of all Poland to the direct incorporation of part of its territory. Still the agreement could be regarded as a positive success. France, which had so often in the past intervened in Polish affairs in her role of Poland's traditional protector, resigned herself to the situation. To Austrian demands for joint action Louis XV answered: 'It is difficult to help Poland from a distance of 500 leagues. I would have desired that she could be kept intact but I can do nothing more than wish.' King Stanislav, who advised the Polish *Sejm* in May 1773 to accept the annexations, reported on his fruitless efforts to secure assistance or even mediation: 'Great Britain, France and Sweden as well as the States-General of the United Provinces had answered that "they were touched by the distress in which we find ourselves but in their expressions of concern they show that the possibility of helping us remains but a wish".' Because of her religious intolerance Poland appeared to be a very backward country, a factor which lessened public sympathy for her. Voltaire could announce that the Russian empress was bringing to Poland the advantages of the Enlightenment. The British secretary of state, Lord Suffolk, informed the envoy at Warsaw at the beginning of October 1772 that the spoliation of his territory earned the king of Poland

35 Political satire in the *Westminster Magazine* of London, August 1774, relating to the first partition of Poland in August 1772.

sympathy, but that at the same time Poland had largely brought her tribulations on herself, by reason of her internal disunity and her fissiparous politics.

A sober assessment must conclude that it was not un-European methods which brought about Poland's collapse but the consequences of enlightened Europe's political theory and power politics. To contemporaries these consequences were revealed in all their clarity in 1795 when – despite all former promises – the partitioning powers decided on the third and final partition of Poland. That the loss of its independence by an entire people and the disappearance of an old and distinctive crown was allowed to occur signified a fissure in the deepest strata of the juridical foundations of the *ancien régime*. Friedrich von Gentz, the German publicist, later a collaborator of Metternich, wrote in 1806 (in a book first published in St Petersburg) that this signified Europe's enfeeblement: 'If the partition of Poland through the misuse of the balance of power system was the first event to lead to a tremendous upheaval in Europe it was also one of the first to reveal the prostration of the spirit, and the decay of active concern for the common interests of states. The silence of France and England, nay, the silence of all of Europe during the planning and perpetration of such a dubious act is as astonishing as the event itself.'

While Russia acquired the duchy of Courland – in which she had long held a decisive influence – by the Third Partition she also annexed the remaining parts of the former territories of the Teutonic Knights in Livonia, which had become Protestant during the Reformation. The three Baltic provinces, called the 'German' provinces because of their cultural character and their representative institutions (although the majority of the inhabitants were Estonians and Letts), provided the strongest link between old Russia and the Europe of the *ancien régime*.

Russian power showed itself to be as formidable in the Balkans as it was in Poland. The war with Turkey in 1768 developed from an unwished-for Turkish intervention in Polish affairs, and was vigorously waged by Russia in the pursuit of specific objectives. As early as November 1763, the British ambassador in St Petersburg, John, earl of Buckinghamshire, predicted that the empress, who in any event would do all in her power to advance Russian commercial interests, would take the first opportunity 'of attempting to recover the right of navigating the Black Sea in Russian vessels'. After great military successes, thanks to which the Russians succeeded in occupying the Crimea, crossing the Danube and advancing into the Balkans, the Porte was forced to make an unconditional peace. By the Treaty of Kutchuk-Kainardji (July 1774) Russia gained a narrow outlet to the Black Sea at the mouth of the Dnieper, and freedom of navigation in the Aegean as well as in the Black Sea, while Turkey had to surrender her suzerainty over the Tartars of the Crimea and Kuban. But Russia's greatest gain, one of the highest political significance, was the double right of intervention on behalf of a newly built Greek Orthodox church in Constantinople and on behalf of the Danubian principalities, Moldavia and Wallachia, which, in addition, were to be permitted to have their own diplomatic representation at the Porte.

The appearance of a Russian fleet in the Mediterranean during the Russo-Turkish war heralded the new claims of the Russian Empire, even before Russia had secured her role as the protector of Orthodoxy in the Balkans. Britain, welcoming the appearance of the Russians in southern Europe as a counterweight to France, assisted the Russian

36, 37 Catherine II deliberately chose her lovers and favourites from among the Russians. Count A. Orlov (right), and Prince G. Potemkin (left) were two of these who remained friends with her throughout her life. Orlov's medal was struck to commemorate his victory at Chesme in 1770 and Potemkin's to commemorate his victories in the Crimea, 1791. Hermitage, Leningrad.

squadron, which was partly officered by British sailors, at its port of call in the south of England: Pitt the Elder was even prepared to give Minorca to the Russians as a base, but this Catherine declined so as to avoid trouble with France. The destruction of the Turkish fleet at Chesme in the Aegean in July 1770 was the Ottoman Empire's heaviest defeat at sea since Lepanto. It created an enormous sensation among contemporaries and was celebrated with joy in 'the educated world' (Goethe). In 1783–84 Catherine II annexed the Crimea. 'It was the first time the Baltic, the Mediterranean and the Atlantic were convulsed by the same event, that a general European crisis developed simultaneously in the Baltic and beyond the Pyrenees, on the Bosporus and along the Atlantic coasts' – thus the German historian Dietrich Gerhard assessed the importance of these events. Catherine's ostentatious and publicity-seeking journey to the Crimea in the early summer of 1787 in the company of the Holy Roman Emperor Joseph II demonstrated the 'new degree of strength' which the Russian Empire had acquired, as Joseph II noted. It was during this journey that the favourite Potemkin, who had been made a prince of the empire by Joseph II in 1776, created the *mise en scène* of extensive colonization and settlement by cleverly arranged 'Potemkin villages'.

71

From the honorary title 'Tavricheskii' bestowed on him by Catherine II the beautiful palace which Potemkin had built for himself in St Petersburg came to be called the Tauride Palace. This, in another connection, became famous in the twentieth century.

That Russia, not France, was now the leading European power was demonstrated not only by her defeat of Poland and her triumph over the Turks but by Denmark's adherence to the Russian system, the Russian guarantee for the Austro-Prussian Peace of Teschen (1779) and Catherine's Declaration of the League of Armed Neutrality (1780), by which the maritime trade of neutral powers was to be protected against interference from Britain during the American War of Independence. In time the Russian proposals were to become part of maritime law. Compared with the genuine possibilities for the expansion of Russian power which Catherine II methodically exploited some of her ideas and projects were decidedly unreal. Among these daydreams – despite intense diplomatic activity over many years from 1782 – was the plan for the restoration of the Greek Empire at Constantinople, in the form of a Russian secondogeniture, a scheme which could have been realized only if the Turks were driven out of Turkey and if the highly improbable consent of Austria was acquired. Even more fantastic was a secret plan which proposed a gigantic empire with Constantinople, Vienna and Berlin as its main cities. That went far beyond the bounds of possibility.

But how contradictory was this powerful empire! The great insurrection of the Cossack Emelyan Pugachev was, in a certain sense, just a new manifestation of the old violent uprisings of the Russian peasants. Pugachev gained control of the Volga and Ural territories (1774). At first he was underestimated by the government but the revolt gave Catherine II a lasting shock. On the eruption of the French Revolution, an event which aroused the empress's indignation, she compared the members of the National Assembly – those *canailles* – with the 'Marquis Pugachev'. The very same comparison reappeared when the highly educated Russian aristocrat A. N. Radishchev published anonymously in St Petersburg (1790) his *Journey from Petersburg to Moscow* – after the pattern of Sterne's *A Sentimental Journey*. This was sharply critical of internal conditions in Russia. The author, Catherine declared, was worse than Pugachev, and the outspoken critic was sent in chains to Siberia. Similar to Radishchev was Nikolai Novikov, at one time secretary of the

Legislative Commission, now a critic whose influence was based on his periodicals which were widely read among the Russian aristocracy. In Russia the ideas of the Enlightenment found their strongest supporters among the freemasons. Their lodges were widespread among the aristocracy and they contributed decisively to the development of a new Russian type, 'an individual westernized not only outwardly but inwardly as well'. 'The English gentry were the model for the Russian aristocracy at the end of the eighteenth century' (M. Raeff). At the same time the obligation of public service became for many of the best of them a commitment to social reform.

When the Enlightenment, to which Catherine had so deeply committed herself, turned from political theory to practice, she became the sharpest critic of these contemporary tendencies. Yet she allowed her grandson to be educated by the Swiss Laharpe, a follower of Locke and Rousseau and a convinced republican whom she called 'M. le Jacobin'. Secure in her position she dismissed as unimportant alarmed representations from French émigrés against her grandson's tutor for she did not realize that the spirit of the age was stronger than monarchic power.

In no other period of history, either before or since, was Russia so closely connected with the rest of Europe as she was during the Napoleonic era. That the Greek Orthodox emperor, Paul I, son and successor of Catherine the Great, should become grand master of the Knights of Malta in 1798 was highly unusual but Russia's expansionist policies and the constant appeals for her intervention by the older European powers gave the framework of her foreign policy the capability to absorb even this. On occasion such requests for an alliance with Russia have perhaps advanced Russia's involvement with Romano-German Europe even more than her own activities. Paul I took part in the Second Coalition against Napoleon on the side of Austria and Britain; two years later he joined with Napoleon against Britain. But in the spring of 1801 he was murdered by a group of his own officers, among them some whose mother tongue was German.

His successor, his son Alexander I, showed his Europeanism in May 1802 in Dorpat where the second university of the Russian Empire was founded, a Protestant German-speaking foundation not only for the Baltic provinces. The twenty-three-year-old emperor was greeted by a speech in French given by Professor G. F. Parrot, a Württemberger of French parentage who in the name of Freedom and

Equality won the emperor's friendship. The German writer of the *Sturm und Drang* period, F. M. Klinger, who as a major-general commanded the Russian Cadet Corps, in a letter to Goethe in 1802 called the young Russian emperor 'the noblest regent in Europe'. Between 1816 and 1819 Alexander I abolished serfdom in Livonia, Estonia and Courland, long before it was possible to do so in the Russian interior. Among the emperor's closest advisers during the early years of the reign was the Polish Prince Adam Czartoryski, who was Russian minister for foreign affairs from 1804 to 1806. In 1803 Russia's third university, the Polish-speaking University of Vilna, was opened. Other Russian universities followed later – Kazan 1804, Kharkov 1805 and St Petersburg 1819.

With the Peace of Tilsit in July 1807 the 'Napoleonic period' of Alexander I's reign began; the alliance of the Eastern Empire with the Western usurper against England, the acquisition by Russia of Swedish Finland with Napoleon's support in 1809 and the continuation of the war with Turkey, concluded with the annexation of Bessarabia in 1812. During these years, M. M. Speransky the highly gifted son of a village priest, who was familiar with French political theory, suggested substantial internal reforms as secretary of state. Their significance, however, derived largely from their bold conception and intellectual range, for only a few of them were ever realized.

When the break between Russia and the Napoleonic Empire finally came in 1812 it ushered in the period of Russia's most intimate relationship with Europe.

As members of Napoleon's *Grande Armée* soldiers from all over Europe came in contact with a sizable part of European Russia. They were able to appreciate its vastness and Moscow's strange beauty as it spread before them, wealthy, deserted and engulfed in flames. They experienced also the hard Russian winter and the Russian people in all their primitiveness; pious, superstitious, cruel and compassionate. An even closer relationship with Russia was established by those foreigners who came to Russia as Napoleon's enemies and the numerous German-speaking officers from the Baltic provinces. Whether or not Europe went to Russia with or against Napoleon Russia came to Europe through the Wars of Liberation; Alexander I as a liberator, Russian officers as comrades, Cossacks – so different from their previous visits to inhospitable parts of Europe – to be gazed at as strange but harmless guests. Each of the three monarchs who made the victorious entry into Paris in 1815, the emperors of Austria and Russia and the king of Prussia, could be seen as a representative of one of the three main Christian confessions. Alexander I attempted to bring the European rulers and their peoples together in a Christian nation ('sous la dénomination de nation chrétienne') for they were 'of the same nation' and 'the Christian nation, essentially one' had no other sovereign but Jesus Christ. Metternich had Alexander's draft of the Holy Alliance amended to exclude those central passages which argued the necessity of a fundamental change in the behaviour of the powers and which carried references to the interests of 'the peoples'.

But Alexander was aiming at more than just a Holy Alliance: he put forward proposals for disarmament and he envisaged a collective security system for Europe in which all could co-operate. His sense of mission was awakened and nourished by the hopes of salvation placed in him by many. The general guarantee agreement which he proposed in 1818 was intended as a 'binding association' of rulers as well as peoples which would benefit the whole 'great European family'. His claim to hegemony was compatible with a highly conscious Europeanism. Possibly no other ruler of a great European state was ever so drawn to the vision of a united Europe as this Russian emperor. That still held true when in the face of increasing revolutionary unrest in Europe – from the autumn of 1819 – he dropped his proposed *charte constitutionelle* for Russia. A remark of his from the summer of 1819 shows that the thought of abdication was in his mind: 'Never before has Europe stood in such need of young sovereigns in the full plenitude of their energies and strength. . . .'

At the conferences and courts Russia was represented not only by the emperor himself but by numerous non-Russians in his service. One of the most characteristic figures among them was the secretary of state and foreign minister, Count Karl von Nesselrode, later vice-chancellor and then imperial chancellor, who for forty years conducted Russian foreign policy. His father was an imperial count from the Catholic Rhineland, his mother a Huguenot. Born on an English ship off Lisbon where his father was Russian envoy and baptized in the Anglican faith, Nesselrode was raised as a Lutheran in Berlin, educated in German cultural circles and was married to a Greek Orthodox Russian, without ever learning to speak Russian correctly. He was a

38, 39, 40 Russia was an active ally against Napoleon and her role was important in bringing about his downfall. Left, marauders from the French army frightened by a Russian peasant. I. Terebeniev, 1812. Hermitage, Leningrad. Below, 'Allied powers unbooting Egalité'. James Gillray, cartoon 1799. Bottom, George Cruikshank, cartoon, Napoleon *en route* to Elba. 23 April 1814. British Museum.

ALLIED POWERS *UN-BOOTING* EGALITE.

41 The Holy Alliance: Emperor Alexander I of Russia, Emperor Franz I of Austria and King Frederick-William III of Prussia. Engraving. Staatsbibliothek, Berlin.

42 Below, Napoleon's army retreating across the Beresina River, 1812. Anonymous painting. Musée de l'Armée, Paris.

doughty upholder of conservative European views and of Russian power interests. Working alongside him as second secretary of state for some years was the constitutionalist Count John Capodistrias from Corfu who had been in Russian service since 1809 and who was later to become first president of an independent Greece. The Corsican Count C. A. Pozzo di Borgo, Russian envoy at Paris from 1814, must also be mentioned as must those Russian envoys from the German nobility in the Baltic provinces such as Count Lieven – son of the imperial governess – in London, Count Stackelberg in Vienna and Count Pahlen in Munich. In Berlin was the Finn, D. Alopaeus, while Anstedt, an Alsatian, was at the *Bundestag* in Frankfurt. During the Congress of Vienna a Russian in the emperor's entourage calculated that of the thirty-seven Russian diplomats present only sixteen had Russian names. Was all this a new wave of foreign predominance in Russia? Russian *amour-propre* was hurt during the patriotic war against Napoleon in 1812 because at first the 'German' Barclay de Tolly held the supreme command of the army. His replacement by the Russian Kutuzov was received with great satisfaction.

As the protector of Orthodoxy the Russian Church resisted the syncretic Pietism of the emperor and Alexander's speech in Warsaw in 1818 inviting the first Polish *Sejm* to give Europe and Russia an example of liberalism in action aroused intense indignation in Russia. It is part of the dialectic of modern European history that both cosmopolitanism with its emphasis on European unity and nationalism, which disrupts that unity, have their origin in European thought, while the structure of the ruling class was everywhere experiencing the same changes. Thus 'Congress Poland', created by the Congress of Vienna, which had reconstituted half of Poland under Russian sovereignty, was no lasting solution. Although Alexander I – unlike his grandmother Catherine II – was willing to allow the Poles their own way of life (he regarded himself as their only friend) the existence of the imperial high commissioner, a high-ranking representative of the emperor called N. N. Novosiltsev, was not allowed for in the *charte constitutionelle* which Alexander had granted the Poles in 1815. And the emperor's brother, the Grand Prince Constantine, who was commander-in-chief of the Polish army often ignored the constitution. The recalcitrant attitude of the second *Sejm* in autumn 1820, during which many Polish patriots formed themselves into secret societies, hurt and distressed Alexander I.

From 1820 at the very latest, the emperor was aware that secret societies were also being formed in Russia, but he made no move to eradicate them. It is possible that he realized that many of the reformist ideas being developed in them had previously had his support and that the conspirators could point to the fact that at an earlier period he had himself raised 'the lamp of freedom'. His brother and successor, Emperor Nicholas I, almost twenty years his junior, was also aware of this. In 1821 the Southern League (in the Ukraine) and the Northern League (in St Petersburg) were formed from various small groups of guards officers. These were secret organizations modelled on foreign societies such as the *Carbonari* and the Prussian *Tugendbund* and combined with old Russian traditions. In a community of young guards officers at St Petersburg, which called itself the 'Holy Artel', an old Novgorodian myth was cultivated; in their draft constitution the National Assembly was to be called by the ancient Russian title, the *vyeche*.

The programme developed by the more radical Southern League reproduced in its preface the ideas of Rousseau, called itself the *Russkaya Pravda* after the oldest Russian code of law and contained traces of nationalism. From the sociological point of view it was an aristocratic revolutionary movement: the plotters belonged to the higher nobility, the landed aristocracy and the hereditary service gentry; various clauses of their constitutional programme show that the authors were oblivious to the interests of the bourgeoisie.

However, these proposals mirror the general change in philosophical and socio-ethical concepts that was manifesting itself among the aristocratic class in Russia. The constitutional programme of the Northern League, in which elements of the American, Spanish and French constitutions were woven together, laid down that no human being should legally belong to another. This demand, it claimed, was based not only on secularized natural law but derived directly from Christian teaching. In accordance with God's will all are well born, for all are born for their own good, all are simply human beings, 'for all are weak and imperfect'. Of course the impressions received by a great number of revolutionary officers in Western Europe during the Wars of Liberation must be seen as a fundamental factor in the development of these societies, and they were also strongly influenced by the revolutions in southern Europe. But the conditions within which an aristocratic opposition could operate passed away with the eighteenth

43 The Decembrist Rising, 26 December 1825. V. F. Timm. Hermitage, Leningrad.

century. However, in their intellectual content the programmes were much more than mere translations from the works of Western European radicals – and the victims were real.

The revolution which broke out after the death of Alexander I in December 1825 and was quelled by Nicholas I, turned the aristocratic Decembrists into Russia's first martyrs for freedom. Among those 126 convicted, five of whom were hanged in July 1826 and the rest exiled to Siberia, were many bearers of old and famous names and sons of princely families. Among those hanged was the political writer K. F. Ryleev. Retribution reached down to those soldiers and non-commissioned officers won over by their officers: eight were condemned to hard labour, almost two hundred were forced to run the gauntlet and hundreds more were transferred to distant garrisons.

The decision of many of the wives of the Decembrists to pay the high price exacted in order to obtain permission to follow their husbands into exile was an example of love and courage: they lost their aristocratic standing with all its privileges and they had to prepare themselves for the grey grind of exile. Among the first women to ask for this permission were the princesses Volkonsky and Trubetskoy. Their action was in itself a political demonstration.

Nicholas I suppressed the revolt and took all the inevitable measures, sentences of death, imprisonment, tighter control of public opinion and increased police surveillance. He was the first ruler of a great European power in the nineteenth century to be confronted with a revolutionary uprising in his own country. The December revolution in Russia preceded the July revolution in France. Russia might appear in the eyes of Western Europeans as the most backward of countries but she had – it seemed – the most advanced aristocracy.

One of the consequences of the suppression of the Decembrist revolt was the reputation acquired by Nicholas I's Russia as being one of Europe's strongest bulwarks against revolutionary movements. This increased her stature among conservative forces in other states. On the other hand liberals saw Russia as the stronghold of reaction and they bitterly attacked her backwardness. In Western Europe Russia was spoken of as being 'Asiatic' or accused of being a 'Chinese despotism', but Russian critics sometimes called their exacting emperor 'Karl Ivanovich' (no Russian can be called Karl) or a 'Russian German' in 'Prussian uniform'.

From the beginning the dominant features of Nicholas I's system of government were militarism and repression. On Sunday mornings the emperor inspected the cadet corps as they mounted guard in the Michael Riding School in St Petersburg, and for a career in the public service there was no better foundation than a commission in the army. But the system's most characteristic institution was the Third Section of His Majesty's Own Chancery, set up in 1826 and embracing the gendarmerie and its superior arm, the secret police. Its function was to control the bureaucracy and to exercise supervision over politics and morals. Although very much open to criticism for its police-state methods of arbitrary denunciation and arrest the Third Section was not quite as bad as its reputation would suggest. Its first head, Alexander von Benckendorff (created a count in 1832), a trusted adviser of the emperor, was upright and independent minded. One of the most deeply rooted evils in Russian life was bribery, rife among the bureaucracy, and all the efforts of the emperor and his advisers failed to eradicate it. The reasons for this failure were many. Generally speaking the bureaucracy fell far short of the task of administering a vast empire. In the first half of the nineteenth century the number of ranking higher officials increased threefold in comparison with the growth in administrative duties. The functionaries in the lower echelons of the service, badly paid, utterly dependent on the emperor and answerable only to him, were generally more interested in

44 Drawing illustrating Gogol's comedy, a satire about Russian bureaucracy, *The Inspector General*, 1836. Narodnaya Biblioteca, Moscow.

safe-guarding their careers than in efficient administration. The aristocracy was unable to act as a counterweight – especially after the Decembrist revolt – because it was never an estate within a social whole, and Russia had no bourgeoisie in the Western European sense. On the other hand the emperor himself lost some of his freedom of action to the growing bureaucracy.

The most characteristic phenomenon of Nicholas's reign was the growth of the multi-graded bureaucracy, the *Chinovnichestvo*, which rose like a wall between the emperor and his peoples. A great Russian writer, Nikolai Gogol, directed his sharpest satire at this situation in his comedy *The Inspector General*. Yet that legendary reactionary, Nicholas I, not only allowed but actually ordered the production of this play and the autocratic, pedantic and uneducated monarch was even broadminded and clever enough to withdraw Russia's greatest writer, Alexander Pushkin, from the attentions of the official censorship and place him under the eye of his own more tolerant personal censorship, even though Pushkin was regarded as being politically unreliable and had sympathized with the Decembrists. Admittedly he was under supervision, but he was also under protection. Pushkin, who died as the result of a duel in 1837, was a writer of European stature who secured for all time Russia's place in the literary firmament. But the exceptional treatment accorded to Gogol and Pushkin brought no basic change in the strict and detailed system of surveillance which so marked Nicholas I's reign. General L. V. Dubbelt, a director of the Third Section, who began his career in 1839 under Benckendorff, once noted that 'here in Russia intellectuals must be treated like apothecaries who have at their disposal remedies and poisons; they are allowed to dispense their learning only by government prescription'. Alexander Herzen – who is dealt with below – observed with deadly irony that 'it is true that censorship contributes greatly to the development of style and mastery of the language'. He also remarked that 'youth, cut off from all activity considered unlawful by the secret police, threw themselves all the more fiercely on reading matter with the result that ideas circulated more rapidly'.

The famous description of Nicholas I's reign as 'thirty years of black frost' is not altogether accurate but it does indicate clearly the layer of administrative suppression. An event of truly European importance – though half-hidden – was the reception in the 1830s and 1840s of Hegelianism and the discussion it aroused. In this case – so different from the period of the Enlightenment – Russian thought rose to the level of contemporary philosophy, not just temporarily but permanently, and ideas appeared which were neither borrowings from abroad nor imitations of foreign theories but which presented a distinct contribution to the development of European thought. This occurrence can be dated to the exact year: in 1837 a whole generation began to read Hegel. In his memoirs Herzen relates how there was 'not one paragraph in the three parts of *Logic*, the two parts of *Aesthetics* or the *Encyclopedia* which was not conquered through fierce debates, often lasting through several nights'. Soon afterwards began the split between the so-called Westernizers, the *zapadniki*, and the Slavophiles but they were unable to ignore their common philosophical and historical background. Both movements produced original thinkers and writers, even if they were partly indebted to foreign mentors – as indeed were Hegel's own opponents, particularly Schelling.

The most important of the Westernizers was Alexander Herzen (Gercen), born the son of a Moscow aristocrat and a middle-class Protestant German mother from what was regarded as an illegitimate union by the Russian Church. As a result Herzen had no Russian surname. He spoke French as his second mother tongue, as indeed did all educated Russian aristocrats, he read and wrote German and in exile he learned English. 'I came to Europe as a foreigner', Herzen wrote in 1849, although a year earlier he had stated that he felt 'at home' in Europe. In the deepest and widest sense this un-bourgeois Russian was more European than any of his fellow European intellectuals. More and more he was inspired by the newly understood historical importance of Russia. 'No sooner awake, we encounter Europe and behold! our natural, semi-wild way of life corresponds more to the European ideal than does the way of life of the civilized Romano-German world. The hope arrived at by the West is our starting-point. We, downtrodden by imperial absolutism, proceed towards socialism. . . .' Among the sureties for Russia's socialist future were – according to Herzen – the village commune and the *artel*. 'The idea of a social revolution', he wrote foresightedly, 'is a Western idea but it does not follow that the people of the West alone are destined to put it into practice.' Perhaps it was to be no more than the West's last will and testament. At the same time Herzen was and remained – in company with the liberals of his time – a defender of personal freedom and of the demand for a freer individuality.

The most profound thinker among the Slavophiles was Alexei Stepanovich Khomiakov. He began his work as a publicist with an answer to *La Russie en 1839* (published in Paris 1843, translated into English and German), the impressions of Russia of a French writer, the Marquis de Custine. Making full use of the very brilliant work of Peter Chaadaev which was also very critical of his country, Custine produced a disparaging account of Russia which drew Khomiakov into print. From 1845 onwards he developed a complete system of religio-philosophical and socio-theological ideas at the heart of which was the teaching of the *sobornost*, the Christian community which he rediscovered in the Russian social tradition.

With great vehemence Khomiakov turned against Western Europe's claim to leadership: Hegelianism – strong in analysis, in synthesis valueless – had 'plumbed the depths of the intellectual abyss on the brink of which philosophizing Germany has stood unawares for such a long time.' After Hegel all attempts to stride into the future along purely philosophical paths had become impossible. 'Up to the present no new spiritual principle has appeared or, for that matter, can appear which is capable of filling that emptiness in the human soul caused by the final decay of the Latin-Protestant principle.' Socialism must fail. Only the consciousness of our native primitive Christianity which is to be found in Russia's peasant class promised salvation. The Balkan Slavs were united with the Russians through their Greek Orthodox faith. But Khomiakov's thought was oriented towards philosophy and theology, rather than politics. It was possible to develop a democratic element from his Slavophilism, and this was, in fact, done by his followers but at the same time it was the source of an intolerant pan-Slavism, from which, however, Khomiakov himself was free. Coming, as they did, from very different sources, Slavophilism differed from the Official Patriotism which one of the most eminent ministers of the Nicholas I period, Sergei Semenovich Uvarov (1834–49 minister of education) defined as Orthodoxy, Autocracy, Nationalism (*narodnost*).

To demonstrate the wealth of ideas with which Russia's educated class came to grips with the problem of 'Russia and Europe' many other names would have to be mentioned. The most daring and most active critics of the regime emigrated – among them Herzen and Bakunin – belonging from then on to 'the emigrés' internationale', in which a new revolutionary European togetherness was given expression and which included Russians.

In the meantime the animosity of the imperial government towards revolution became more and more pronounced. After the outbreak of the July revolution in Paris Nicholas I would have liked to attack France, which was of course impossible, and he refused to address Louis-Philippe as 'frère', the usual form of address among monarchs. In November of the same year, 1830, the Polish revolution erupted in Warsaw. This was suppressed by Russian troops, the imperial government reacting with savage punishments, the assimilation of Poland's eastern territories and a curtailment of Polish autonomy. For a while Nicholas I thought of giving up Poland – as notes in his own hand dating from June 1831 show – once military victory over the rebels had been gained, and contenting himself for the future with securing the frontiers. But he soon dropped that idea. The flood of Polish refugees intensified the anti-Russian feeling of the 'emigrés' internationale'.

The distinction between the administration of the Russian *gouvernements* and the Baltic provinces was acknowledged during the reign of Alexander I. Serfdom had been abolished only in Livonia, Estonia and Courland. Nicholas I's agrarian policy entrenched this distinction.

In Livonia the government supported the reform policy of the liberal part of the gentry by recognizing in law that land under cultivation by the peasant communes should be left to them. For the Russian peasant there was as yet no sweeping reform. There were only some marginal improvements in the safeguarding of their rights, despite the fact that the emperor had set up numerous consultative committees to study the question. In 1845 that savage instrument of corporal punishment, the knout, was finally abolished; the knout, a vicious leather strap was to disappear for ever; orders went out that these instruments of torture were to be buried in the earth. Although corporal punishment was retained – as it was in England and elsewhere – the 'Russian knout' at last became an anachronism.

Russia's predominance in Europe affected only certain areas, and in different ways. It was most noticeable in Germany where the Russian imperial house established through its marriage alliances a dynastic clientele. For over a century the German princely houses provided Russia with its empresses. After Catherine II came princesses from Hesse, Württemberg, Baden, Prussia (Charlotte, sister of King Frederick William IV, and of the future Emperor William I, married Nicholas in 1817) and from Hesse-Darmstadt. Grand Prince Mikhail, one of Nicholas's brothers, married a Württemberger princess who, under her Greek Orthodox name of Helene Pavlovna, established a famous *salon* in her St Petersburg palace. From the political point of view the marriages of Russian princesses were even more important. Through these Russian influence permeated the German courts. Three of Paul I's daughters and two of Nicholas I's daughters were married to reigning German princes. In Prussia a feeling of dependence on Russia existed – especially from 1850 when Russian pressure forced Prussia to accept a return to the *status quo* in her dispute with Austria over hegemony in Germany. Count Robert von der Goltz noted in 1852 that: 'We live in the province of New Russia or West Russia and are governed by hereditary Stadholders from the house of Hohenzollern.' Looking back over the reign of Nicholas I Bismarck expressed the same opinion: 'during his reign we lived as Russian vassals'.

It is understandable that liberals had the impression that Russia was seeking to establish a universal monarchy. The Czech spokesman Francis Palácky defended his refusal to participate in the Frankfurt Assembly in 1848 partly on the grounds that the Austrian Empire had to be preserved as a defence against the possibility of a 'Russian universal monarchy' as 'Europe's shield and bulwark against Asiatic elements of all kinds'.

Little more than a year later – in summer 1849 – the intervention of Russian troops in Hungary showed that Austrian imperial power depended on Russian help for the suppression of the national democratic movement. Nicholas I made it a point to invade not just with auxiliary troops but with a massive force, so as to score a decisive victory over the revolutionaries. In this several motives intertwined: fear that the whole European order, as set up in Vienna in 1815, would collapse, the revival of the Polish danger and a strong personal determination to strengthen the monarchic principle so as to preserve the existing order in Europe. The Russian troops were completely victorious in Hungary. But contemporaries questioned the possibility of isolating a whole empire from the 'air of revolution'. 'Russia's invasion of the neighbouring Hungarian republic is the open door through which the revolutionary spirit has flashed past and this spirit will not be idle behind the backs of the invaders' (K. Heinzen, 1849). Writing in the same vein against the Russian 'Quarantine establishments' for keeping out Western intellectual influences (especially the repressive policies of the universities) Herzen wrote: 'It's as vain as

45 Troops returning to France in 1855 after fighting in the Crimea. Painting by Y. Massé. Musée de Carnavalet, Paris.

trying to stop the sun's light by a frontier post.' This reflects the nineteenth-century belief that ideas possessed a power and independence stronger than that of all institutions and organizations.

Russia's active policy in the Balkans caused mounting anxiety both in Western Europe and in Austria. After the victorious Turkish War of 1828–29 Russian diplomacy succeeded, in the Treaty of Ungiar-Skelessi in 1833, in making a defensive agreement with Turkey whereby the closure of the Straits was to be handled in accordance with Russian interests. From 1835 a British embassy secretary in Constantinople, the Scot David Urquhart, published in the *Portfolio* documents proving that Russia's expansionist policies were directed against Constantinople, thereby undermining the whole of Europe. These same arguments were used by Marx and Engels in their struggle against Imperial Russia.

The Straits Convention of 1841, in which the great powers and the Porte agreed to the closure of the Dardanelles and the Bosporus to foreign warships in time of peace, did not eliminate tension. On the contrary, Nicholas I, convinced that the Turkish Empire was on the point of collapse, intensified his efforts to gain a controlling interest in its liquidation. And in 1853 he was drawn into a new war with Turkey, having through the exertion of unsuccessful pressure on the Porte placed himself in a position from which he could not withdraw without loss of prestige. Britain, France and, eventually Sardinia went to Turkey's aid. Britain's declaration of war, dated 28 March 1854, spelled out – after an *exposé* of the course of the negotiations – her general position: Queen Victoria wished 'to save Europe from the preponderance of a Power which has violated the faith of treaties, and defies the opinion of the civilized world. . . .' This was more than a rebuff of some of Russia's claims, it was the rejection of a system over which Russia claimed to exercise a predominating influence.

The war became the Crimean War when the allies landed in the Crimea and the bloody struggles there played a decisive role. The war was already lost when Nicholas I died in March 1855 even though the Malachov-Kurgean fort, on which the fate of Sevastopol depended, held out for another six months.

Nicholas's successor, his son Alexander II, drew the necessary conclusions from this defeat: in March 1856 he concluded the Treaty of Paris. The new reign brought change and renewal to Russia, opening a new chapter in the relationship between 'Russia' and 'Europe'.

IV THE ASIAN HORIZON:
COLONIAL POWER – WORLD POWER

Of all the great European powers Russia had the most compact colonial empire. Muscovy's systematic colonization of Siberia from the second half of the sixteenth century onwards may have been quickened by the fear that either the English or the Dutch might gain a foothold in northern Asia; for after Chancellor's enterprising voyage another search for a direct route to Asian markets could not be discounted. The Russians, however, were no strangers to the territories beyond the Urals: since the end of the fifteenth century they had exchanged envoys with the khans of Tiumen while various tribes of the Ob region already paid tribute to the Muscovite tsars. After the conquest of the khanates of Kazan and Astrakhan in the 1550s Muscovy was in a position to contemplate further advances into Asia.

Soviet research has shown that the actual spearhead of Russian colonization in Siberia was furnished by peasants and Cossacks. Without the pioneering skills of various classes the surprisingly rapid results of Russian expansion in Siberia could not have been achieved.

The Stroganovs, a family of *entrepreneurs* specially favoured by the tsars, were responsible for one of the earliest and most effective thrusts. From fisheries, saltworks, trade and forestry in the Kama valley in Northeast Russia they had amassed not only an enormous fortune but had established a regional ascendancy which allowed them the right to maintain their own armed force. When Stroganov interests came under attack from trans-Ural tribes in 1581 they sent a detachment of troops under the command of a Cossack hetman of unknown origin, Yermak Timofeevich, across the Urals in pursuit. By October 1582 the Stroganov expedition had occupied Kashlyk, the small settlement on the Irtysh river where the West Siberian khan, Kuchum, had his headquarters. Moscow, taking over from the Stroganovs, sent troops who completed the conquest of the khanate in 1598 by gaining a decisive victory over Kuchum. During these decades Muscovy secured her position in western Siberia by the construction of various strongholds. The foundation of Tobolsk in 1587 was followed by that of Pelym in 1593, Verkhoturye in 1598 and

Tomsk in 1604. The native population, made up of different ethnic groups practising various pagan cults, were brought under Russian tribute. The most important of these was the fur tribute, the *yasak*, for the constant supply of sable pelts was Muscovy's main interest in the region.

In a similar way eastern Siberia was joined to Russia by the middle of the seventeenth century. In the wake of the Russian advance eastwards Yeniseisk was founded in 1619, followed by Krasnoyarsk in 1628, Ilimsk in 1630, Yakutsk in 1632, Nerchinsk in 1654 and Irkutsk in 1661. A Cossack force penetrated the Kamchatka peninsula in 1697. By the end of the seventeenth century the whole of northern Asia right across to the Pacific was under Russian rule. From 1637 Siberia was administered by a central authority in Moscow, the *Sibirskii prikaz*. Although only sparsely dotted with Russian settlements, Siberia was traversed by trade caravans and embassies which connected European Russia with China and the Central Asian khanates of Khiva and Bokhara. It was an immense territory, thinly peopled by Ugrians, Samoyeds, Tungus, Turki tribes and others, but rich in natural resources. In extent it was neither a province not a *gouvernement* but an *imperium*, 'in which there were more than forty rivers larger than the Danube' (as a Bosnian-born official of Peter the Great wrote in 1726).

The Russians appeared in Asia as Europeans and Christians, with administrative procedures developed in Moscow and with skilful techniques of exploitation. Superior to the natives culturally, they brought with them Christian missionaries. Although there was a metropolitan for the whole of Siberia from 1668 – centred at Tobolsk – this was not sufficient for the task facing the Church. The most important non-Christian cults were various forms of Shamanism, Buddhist Lamaism and Islam. Peter the Great tried by every means to further missionary work, but by the fall of Imperial Russia the full Christianization of Siberia had not been accomplished.

The Russian drive into Manchuria in the mid-seventeenth century brought Muscovy, and later Imperial Russia, into direct contact with the Chinese Empire. Clashes over the lines of demarcation between their spheres of influence ended with the Russian withdrawal from the Amur basin, regularized in the Treaty of Nerchinsk in 1689. This was China's first treaty with a European power and it safeguarded

Russian sovereignty in eastern Asia while laying a new foundation for Russo-Chinese trade.

Western Europe's interest in *chinoiserie* was known: the fashion for Chinese porcelain, imported in large quantities since the seventeenth century; for Chinese ornamentation, artistic *motifs* and decorative styles brought a strange world within reach. Catholic missionaries were working in China from the end of the sixteenth century and by the beginning of the seventeenth Jesuits had gained access to the imperial court at Peking. The treaty negotiations at Nerchinsk in 1689 were an early instance of global cultural involvement. There Europe completed the circle; for the Russian negotiators found themselves confronted with French and Portuguese Jesuits on the Chinese side and the definitive text of the treaty was drawn up in Latin. Russia had long been familiar with the highly specialized products of Chinese industry; precious materials such as damask and satin, porcelain services and tea were imported by caravan across Siberia into European Russia. In exchange furs, leather, linen and axes were exported to China. Russia, however, was uninterested in the imitation of Chinese cultural modes, even though contact with China did not have to be maintained by sea.

Already in Muscovite times the authorities were aware of the routes to India through Central Asia. Peter the Great was fascinated by the possibilities of this line of thought throughout his reign without, however, falling for the fantastic projects which were afterwards attributed to him. Obviously, his interest was in the formation of a direct trade connection with India along the land route through Persia or Khiva and Bokhara. But it did not materialize; for British diplomacy became restive. The short, successful war against Persia, during which Peter the Great put his foot on Asian soil – admittedly only on the edge – for the first and only occasion in his life (in the summer of 1721) brought Russia a short-lived territorial gain by the Caspian Sea. The acquisition of Baku, at first only temporary, was of far greater importance. Peter the Great gave his support to the scientific expeditions to Siberia of the Danzig doctor, Messerschmidt, as well as to Vitus Bering's search for a sea passage between Asia and America.

Russia's superior attitude towards the indigenous nomadic tribes of Asia owed nothing to her acquisition of Western European techniques or to her assimilation into the European state system. Peter the

Great was no advocate of 'European solidarity' against Asia. At several points in Asia he came up against representatives of other European powers – in China and Persia – and his concerted drive for distant markets could have brought him into conflict with different European powers at any time. Indeed it can be said that Russia's enormous Asian territories and her colonization there was one of the factors which never let the emperor forget that, much as he might consider himself a pupil of 'Old Europe', he represented a power which, in itself, was independent of Europe. After Peter's death the boundaries of Russia's Central Asian territory were secured by forts and fortified *limes* but it was a slow development. Following the absorption of the Kazachs of Uzbek the town of Orenburg was founded in 1731. In the same year the naval base of Okhotsk was established on the Pacific coast. Russia's powerful position in Asia was known in Western Europe, enough at least for her to be called in a German dictionary in 1782 'Europe's pride and Asia's fear'. In the Pacific region the thrust of Russian enterprise carried beyond the boundaries of the Continent from the 1780s. Russians opened up the Alaskan fur trade and, in competition with British maritime expansion on the Pacific coast, took possession of Alaska. The Russian-American Company, granted a patent by Paul I in 1799, was empowered to extend Russian territory in America by the acquisition of further regions as yet unsettled. Russia's notification of this to the European chancelleries brought home to all that she had joined the ranks of the inter-continental colonial powers.

The value of Alaska, however, fell short of expectations: attempts to extend Russian rule southwards along the Pacific coast of America, possibly to occupy California and the Hawaiian Islands, failed. In the first place the determined advance of the United States to the Pacific Ocean blocked the Russians, the financial profits of the Russian-American Company declined and Russian settlers in this far distant land were very few. After years of discussions the Washington Agreement of 1867 resulted in the sale of Alaska and the Aleutian Islands to the United States for 7·2 million dollars. That the strategic importance of this territory in the missile age would far outweigh its economic value could not have been foreseen.

The sale of Russian America did not herald, by any means, a withdrawal of Russia from the Far East. On the contrary, the urgent need for a build-up of Russian power on the Asian mainland was among the arguments advanced in Russia for the sale. Nikolai Muraviev, governor-general of eastern Siberia from 1847 to 1861, launched out on an extension of Russia's Far Eastern empire which was to have very important consequences for the European powers. The foundation of Nikolaevsk (1850) on the mouth of the Amur opposite Sakhalin was followed by the erection of the stronghold of Khabarovsk (1854), which in the course of the following hundred years was to become an important city. In 1858 the Russo-Chinese Treaty of Aigun gave Russia the Amur basin. Two years later the Chinese government confirmed the agreement and ceded, in addition, the Ussuri region. In the same year a military post bearing the imperialistic though romantic name of Vladivostok, 'Lord of the East', was erected at the furthest end of the empire. By 1885 it had become one of Russia's four first-rank naval bases.

The extension of Russian power in the Far East was, like her expansion in Central Asia, entirely different from the earlier opening-up and conquest of Siberia, particularly as it could be only a matter of time before the empire would come into contact with the zones of interest of other European powers. When and where that occurred would depend on a number of factors.

The penetration of Central Asia was interpreted, at first, as a 'hunt for frontiers': this was the way the Russian foreign minister, Prince Gorchakov, explained it in November 1864, claiming that the victorious power was obliged to push forward its frontiers right up to those of another state, because this offered the best guarantee for the preservation of order. In Russia's opinion the khanates of Kokand, Bokhara and Khiva did not offer this security. From the Syr-Darya Line, erected and fortified in 1854, the conquest of Turkestan was begun in 1864. A year later Tashkent, the biggest city in Central Asia, was captured and in 1867 the *gouvernement general* of Turkestan was formed. The first governor-general, General Constantine von Kauffmann, occupied Samarkand in 1868. This fabled city, known to the ancient Greeks, had become, under Arabic rule, one of the main centres of Islamic culture and it contained the impressive mausoleum of Timur (Tamerlane). Bokhara and Khiva (1873) accepted Russian sovereignty. In 1876 the fertile Fergana valley was overrun and incorporated in the *gouvernement general* of Turkestan.

East of the Caspian Sea, the Russians were equally successful in their dealings with the Turkomans. After General Mikhail Skobelev's victory at Geok-Tepe (1881) the region of Transcaspia was formed and in 1897 was incorporated in Turkestan. Russia's occupation of the oasis of Merv in 1884 brought her near the outposts of British India in Afghanistan, leading to a crisis in Anglo-Russian relations in 1885.

Of all Russia's wars of conquest the age-long struggle in the Caucasus was most important, perhaps, in making the Russians aware of their European identity, not least because of the high quality of Russian writing; for Pushkin, Lermontov and Tolstoy have transmuted this struggle into eternal memory. That was made possible by the intellectual and sociological conditions of the nineteenth century, which brought together here many stimuli; the newly discovered world of the mountaineers and the romantic conflict between the superior airs of Russia's Greek Orthodox ruling class and the heroic resistance of the Moslem Caucasians under their famous, almost legendary leader, Imam Shamyl.

The Russian advance in the Caucasus in the eighteenth century also began from a line of fortifications, the so-called Caucasian Line which after the incorporation of the Crimea was again pushed forward. In 1784 the fortress of Vladikavkaz, 'Lord of the Caucasus' (now called Ordzhonikidze), was erected, the name probably serving as a prototype for Vladivostok. The Russian protectorate of the Caucasus was formed in 1785 and Christian Georgia became part of Russia in 1801. From then on one khanate after another was taken over by the Russians. In the mountains guerilla war continued for more than a generation, even beyond the capture of Schamyl in 1859, but, inevitably, the fight for freedom in the Caucasus was crushed.

In the history of Russian colonial administration in Asia a distinction must be made not only between the different historical phases but between the geographical extremes, ranging from the icy tundra in the north to the dry steppe in the south. In the same way the cultural differences existing among the various peoples must be taken into account.

During the reign of Peter the Great and for a century afterwards Siberia carried no weight in the Russian Empire. For a long time it remained untouched by the reforms being initiated in Russia, being valued only from a fiscal point of view. From the seventeenth to the eighteenth century the Russian population of Siberia was 80,000–100,000 males (including male children). It seems certain that even

46, 47 'Defeat' by V. Vereshiagin, a fanciful account of the successful war against the khan of Bokhara. Right, the gateway to the Caucasus. Engravings from Biancardi, *La Russia . . .* , 1877. British Museum.

48 Meeting of the Confederated Princes of Circassia on the bank of the Urin. Lithograph from an engraving by Johann Gottlieb Georgi in *Beschreibung aller Nationen des Russischen Reichs*, 1799, published in E. Spencer, *Travels in Circassia*, London, 1838. British Museum.

then Russians outnumbered natives in this thinly populated land – as far as contemporary opportunities for statistical analysis justify such conclusions. The so-called soul revisions show a steady increase in the Russian population in Siberia, from 169,000 Russians in the first soul revision in 1719 to 412,000 in the fifth revision in 1795, the relative proportion of Russians to the population as a whole remaining at 70 per cent. According to Soviet research the peasant element in the Russian population rose from 60·3 per cent to 82 per cent in this period.

The traditional conception of administrative office as *kormlenie*, literally feedings, a means of self-enrichment, lingered on much longer in the Russian administration of Siberia than in European Russia. On the one hand there were numerous opportunities for advancing personal interests, while on the other there were the great difficulties of exercising supervision. The officials, both high and low, who had mandatory powers commensurate with their rank, were in a position to defraud the exchequer as they levied the pelt tribute and supervised the trade with China. As a deterrent from such peculation Peter the Great publicly hanged Prince Gagarin, the first governor of Siberia, in 1721 in St Petersburg, exhibiting his corpse for a month. Gagarin had been found guilty of large-scale embezzlement. It was possible to check such abuses by the dispatch of special commissioners on tours of inspection, but the evil could not be eradicated entirely, and it remained almost a characteristic of Siberian life until well into the nineteenth century. There were exceptions of course: one such was the governor of Tobolsk F. I. Soymonov (1757–63) who left behind him a reputation for honesty and public-spiritedness. I. B. Pestel (father of the Decembrist), who held the office of governor-general of all Siberia for thirteen years (1806–19) but lived almost all that time at St Petersburg, turned a blind eye to the highly dubious dealings of one of his favourites to whom he had relinquished his duties, but eventually Pestel was removed from office. His successor was M. M. Speransky (1819–21) who had been exiled and later rehabilitated. He not only uncovered some unbelievable abuses but with the help of some of his assistants worked out a reform of the Siberian administration which greatly helped to stimulate native production and particularly encouraged free enterprise. In 1822 the immense territory was divided into two provinces, with lasting effect.

That Siberia had a right to her own development was a thought which only slowly penetrated the official mind. In this respect the construction of the Trans-Siberian Railway was epoch-making for the territory's development. In 1891 work began simultaneously in Chelyabinsk and in Vladivostok, two points 4,375 miles apart, and despite great technical difficulties proceeded rapidly. By 1900 3,427 miles of the 5,000-mile railway were already in use and the remainder was finished in 1904. Soviet historians have rightly pointed out that at the time this project was without comparison anywhere in the world. The initiative, finance and technical planning came from European Russia. One of the most important aspects of the enterprise was the Russian government's refusal to allow the use of foreign capital in its financing. The whole project was under government control, in accordance with the protectionist policies of Witte, then finance minister. The success of the Russians in avoiding the lengthy detour around Manchuria and the direct link-up with Vladivostok through Chinese territory will be examined in another context.

The encouragement of immigration from European Russia was the Siberian administration's main task in the decades before the Revolution. The figures are impressive: during 250–300 years of Russian rule up to the end of the nineteenth century the Russian population of Siberia rose to four millions out of a total population of seven millions. This number, according to estimates, more than doubled in the two decades before World War I. Between 1907 and 1909 more than one and a half million Russians emigrated to Siberia. The administrative apparatus of the resettlement authority rose from 800 to 3,000 officials in five years. Even so the greater proportion of settlers went on their own initiative, without any State assistance.

Only by this increase in population could production have increased so as to compare favourably with that of the good soil conditions of the temperate zone. At this time the government thought of the territory almost solely in terms of agricultural production. But serious problems arose concerning the transport of grain. Export of wheat to the south was prohibited by Chinese embargo policies; to the east it was blocked by Manchurian and American competitors, in the west there was only the possibility of overcoming the customs duties which protected the production of European Russia. To take advantage of the great rivers flowing north would mean overcoming

49 Russian railway station in the Far East. Engraving from E. Ukhtomsky *Travels in the Far East of Nicholas II, Emperor of Russia*, 1896. British Museum.

natural obstacles and interesting Western European buyers in the Arctic trade routes. Provided more great railways were constructed there was the possibility of markets in Russia's Central Asian possessions. A railway for southern Siberia running parallel to the main line was planned; for it would have strategic value as well. Gold-panning in the Lena river, which up to the Revolution was operated by a company in which 70 per cent of the capital was English, promised a great future. But a satisfactory exploitation of the mineral resources and the aquatic powers was only possible by the development of production techniques; this belongs to the Soviet era.

For the development of a 'Siberian' consciousness among the Russian population in Siberia one group of the inhabitants became more and more important not because of their number but in a political sense: these were the political exiles. For these inhospitable territories were already being used as an area of banishment in the Muscovite period. A similar policy was pursued under the empire. It is difficult to quote numbers for the early period, but according to Swedish prisoners of war in the Petrine period disgraced dignitaries were exiled to Siberia, not a few of them dying there. They were followed by prominent critics of social conditions during the period of absolutism. With the rise of widespread revolutionary movement which posed dangers to the government, life and soul destroying punishments which were more appropriate for criminals than for political prisoners were also imposed. Their weeks-long journey to Siberia, fettered in irons, was graven on the consciousness of those Russians with whom they came in contact *en route*. It is indeed part of the Russian experience. Siberia, the place of exile, entered into the Russian soul, even acquiring an international significance.

The greatest sensation was caused by the banishment of more than a hundred Decembrists; for they were all members of the aristocracy. At first they were treated like convicts, being set to hard labour, some of them to work underground in mines. Later they were allowed to settle in Siberia under more or less difficult conditions, as it took years of work to ease their lot. The Decembrists in the prison of Chita, east of Lake Baikal, set up an *artel* in order to divide equally among themselves those comforts sent by their families. Here again the old Russian tradition of self-help blossomed. Their intellectual life found an outlet in a 'penitentiary academy' which they set up. In time many of them took up questions concerned with Siberian conditions. It was from Decembrist circles that the demand arose from the 1840s onwards for the equal treatment of Siberia within the Russian Empire. From

50 Railway building in the Siberian forest, from Ukhtomsky, *Travels . . .* , 1896. British Museum.

51 Siberian exiles at Sakhalin. Photograph from De Windt's *New Siberia*, 1896.
British Museum.

them, too, came the argument that only the abolition of its colonial status could give the territory the impetus towards development which it needed.

Following the Decembrists came other generations of political exiles. After 1830 the great mass of Polish exiles, then the *Petrashevtsy* (1849–50), members of the revolutionary circle which gathered around M. V. Petrashevsky, among whom was no less a figure than the writer Dostoyevsky who spent four years in the prison at Omsk, afterwards serving as a soldier in Semipalatinsk until 1859. These years of suffering in Siberia were to be fundamental for his later work. After the Polish rising in 1863 more than 22,000 Poles were sent to Siberia. Numerous groups of Russian revolutionaries followed, about 4,000 in the 1880s alone. Unrest, opposition and attempts at escape were answered with force, and capital punishment by the regime was not unknown. No longer was Siberia the land of quiet suffering.

Living conditions for political prisoners varied from case to case and from group to group. During Lenin's years of Siberian exile (1897–1900) he was able to work intensively in scientific theory, illegally on practical political work, after a short stay in Krasnoyarsk in the village of Shushenskoe on the upper Yenisei, not far from the Chinese frontier. Bolsheviks as well as Mensheviks were able to engage in political work in their place of exile in Siberia. Prominent among the Mensheviks was their leader I. G. Tsereteli, who after six years of solitary confinement in the penitentiary of Alexandrovsk, in the Nerchinsk region, was able to form a political centre in the place of his 'settlement' near Irkutsk in eastern Siberia and to engage in intellectual work there. One of the natural paradoxes of Russian history is that Russia helped to civilize parts of Asia not alone through her ponderous administration but by the consistent deportation of revolutionaries to Siberia. Through the work of the American journalist, George Kennan, *Siberia and the Exile System* (London 1891) the shocking conditions of Siberian exile became known all over the world. In 1885 the author, who spoke excellent Russian, visited prisons and places of exile in Siberia, accompanied by an artist. Speaking to prisoners, officials and other exiles he observed many facets of Siberian life and formed a balanced, expert and critical opinion which has contributed much to the negative assessment of the Russian system of government in the English-speaking world. His

52 A marching exile party.
Engraving from George Kennan,
Siberia and the Exile System, 1891.
British Museum.

description ended with the resigned wish: 'I hope, with all my heart, that the Siberian exile system may be abolished; but I greatly fear, nevertheless, that it will remain, for many years, one of the darkest blots upon the civilization of the nineteenth century.'

In Central Asia Russia came into contact with a strange though ancient and highly developed culture, so different from her experience in Siberia. The building of the railways opened up many areas. Immediately after Transcaspia had been occupied the Russian government began laying down the railway, mainly for strategic reasons. By 1886 it had reached Merv and in 1888 Samarkand, from which a branch line was extended to Tashkent (1898).

Russian colonial administration in Central Asia suffered from much the same defects as in Siberia. Here, too, one of the few methods of supervision employed was the sudden inspection by an imperial representative of high rank armed with full mandatory powers. One of these trusted civil servants was Count Constantine von Pahlen, whose father was Russian minister of justice during the 1870s. In 1908 Pahlen was sent to inspect the province of Turkestan, which included Transcaspia. As well as finding instances of integrity and responsibility among officials he found, too, evidence of arbitrary behaviour and

53 Meeting of political exiles. Engraving from Kennan, *Siberia . . .* , 1891.

widespread corruption. But comparing the official worlds of colonial powers in Africa and Asia he was led to the conclusion that these administrations were no less corrupt than that of Russia. He saw clearly the cause of this state of affairs and thanks to his gift of observation and his independent judgment his opinions carried some weight. In his memoirs he wrote: 'The entry of Russia into Central Asia, followed by the introduction of European methods and civilization, brought a breath of fresh air to a land despoiled and impoverished by centuries of Asian despotic rule. . . . Slavery was brought to an end; the arbitrary legislation of the Khans, Emirs, and their puppets, the Beks . . . was superseded by Russian law, under which all the inhabitants, irrespective of their standing, were equal.' By 1922 the dark side of the picture of Russian colonial rule, which he had so clearly seen at an earlier period, had brightened. But it must be said that in many cases it was the Russian regime which brought modern European principles and standards of justice into this ancient oriental world.

During these decades when the Russian economy was leaping forward the capitalistic methods by which the Russian government, the crown and private interests advanced economic growth in these new territories were thoroughly European in character. But the interplay of economic and political factors in the imperialistic and capitalistic phase of Russia's expansion in Central Asia and the Far East must be seen in a global setting. This is discussed in the next chapter. Here it is enough to say (in general agreement with B. H. Sumner) that just these tendencies which awakened enmity and criticism among competitors and rivals and which brought into circulation again many outworn anti-Russian clichés were an expression of Russia's progressive Westernization, whereby through the mixture of strong and old and rapidly developing new forces the image was of 'a many-coloured amalgam'. In almost all spheres of life in the empire there was 'an uneasy clash between the old and the new, between different mentalities: the European and the Asiatic . . .': 'all jostled each other, the old and the new, as if in a kaleidoscope.' These contradictions were not only a characteristic feature of the capitalistic age as such but were also an expression of historical problems which were specifically Russian. And because Russia was a colonial power they were felt all the more as Russia grew into a world power. Of course one must always distinguish between what is 'European' and what is 'Asiatic'. 103

V RUSSIA IN THE EUROPEAN POWER SYSTEM

In the two generations between the ending of the Crimean War (1856) and the beginning of the Revolution (1917) sweeping changes occurred in Russia as in most other European countries, but in Russia these changes went deeper and took longer to achieve than elsewhere. Their nature demands a new evaluation of Russia's relationship with the other European states.

The internal transformation of Russia brought about by structural changes, modernization and reform will be dealt with later. Here Russia's standing as a power among the other powers must be examined.

Her military defeat in the Crimean War and the peace conditions imposed upon her by the victorious Western powers did not cause her to retreat into isolationism. Indeed two clauses of the Treaty of Paris of 30 March 1856 brought Russia into closer contact with the other European powers than ever before: Article VIII stipulated the mediation of the other signatory powers in the event of a disagreement between Turkey and any of the other powers. But Russia forfeited that right of intervention in the affairs of the Danubian principalities acquired by her in 1774 as well as her claim to 'exclusive protection' in return for a general guarantee given by all the signatory powers (Art. XXII). She lost, too, the control of the Danube delta and with it control over river navigation. Even more humiliating for a great power with such self-esteem was her enforced acceptance of the neutralization of the Black Sea and the demilitarization of its coastline by the so-called Black Sea clauses of the treaty. (Art. XI, XIII, XIV.)

The Treaty of Paris was not merely a war settlement; Austria and Prussia, both noncombatants, were among the signatories. The peace conference presupposed the continued existence of the old *Concert Européen* and expressly allowed the Porte to share in its advantages. In a separate treaty Britain, France and Austria agreed to treat the violation of the terms of the Treaty of Paris as a *casus belli*. The secure legal and political foundations in which the settlement was embedded made it difficult for a defeated and enfeebled Russia to bring about a revision of the articles of the treaty. But, despite the difficulties, the Russian regime, represented by a new emperor, Alexander II, and a new foreign minister, Prince Gorchakov, made its revision the primary aim of their foreign policy.

Alexander II was more flexible than his father, Nicholas I, but he was also a much weaker character. Through his mother he was a grandson of Frederick William III of Prussia and a nephew of the king of Prussia and later German emperor William I. For his mother's homeland he had a filial, even sentimental, affection although this was never allowed to interfere with the set course of Russian foreign policy, on which the emperor was at one with his foreign minister. Born in 1798, Prince Alexander Gorchakov, in spite of some obvious defects of character, his overweening vanity being much spoken of, was one of the most brilliant exemplars of Russian diplomacy. A member of one of those princely families whose ancestry was more distinguished than that of the imperial house – he traced his descent from Rurik – he inherited a very different background from his mother, though this was not to have any influence on his behaviour. She was a member of Baron von Fersen's family, which had risen to prominence in the service of Sweden while her mother, a Tiesenhausen, belonged to one of the oldest families in the Baltic provinces. Given a solid classical education at the imperial lyceum at Tsarskoe Selo 'this sceptic, exceptionally well educated for a Russian' (K. von Schlözer) had a rare ability in the formulation of policy statements, allied to such a finesse in the expression of nuances that many of his dispatches were minor masterpieces. Spirited and witty as well, he acquired a particular reputation for his pointed *bons mots*.

During the last great Polish uprising in 1863 Gorchakov rejected the intervention of Austria, Britain and France on behalf of the Poles quite in the style of oldfashioned European sovereignty. All of them appealed to 'Europe', though their conception of Europe varied from one to another. Bismarck, who in the Alvensleben Convention of February 1863 promised support to Russia in the suppression of the revolt, regarded a quick dampening of the rebellion as being 'in the interests of Europe'. Against this the British envoy pleaded the interests of an equally fictitious 'Europe'.

Russia's dilemma lay in the fact that while she wanted to preserve the equilibrium established in Central Europe by the Congress of Vienna in 1815 she could loosen the iron clamps which bound her to

54 Christmas party in St Petersburg. Engraving from Biancardi, *La Russia . . .* , 1877.

the provisions of the Treaty of Paris only by disturbing that balance. In 1866 Gorchakov tried, first of all, to prevent the destruction of the European balance and the break-up of the German Bund by Prussia through the united diplomatic intervention of the Western powers at Berlin, but when Napoleon III sought to gain more for France through a direct agreement with Prussia, Gorchakov decided on a similar policy. Looked at from this point of view the considerable addition to Prussia's power won by her victory over Austria in 1866, the dissolution of the German Bund and the setting-up of the North German Bund was secured by France's refusal to accept an alliance with Russia which would include her compliance with the demand for a revision of the Treaty of Paris. Prussia, on the other hand, was quite willing to make concessions.

During the Franco-Prussian War of 1870 a similar situation arose, though this time in a changed political setting; for the French had been defeated and the Germans were now in a position of strength. In August 1870 both Alexander II and Gorchakov declared that Europe's hour had come. In conversation with the Prussian envoy Alexander insisted that the peace conference would have to set itself the task of rebuilding a viable European order while Gorchakov let it be understood that – as Europe 'was lifted from her hinges by this war' –

many matters of moment would have to be discussed, including those dealt with in the Treaty of Paris. This meant that Russia's participation in a European congress would depend on the readiness of the other powers to abrogate the Black Sea clauses. When Britain, who had invited Russia's intervention as one of the neutral powers, refused to support her demands for the revision of the Treaty of Paris, Gorchakov declined to participate in the conference. On 31 October 1870 he announced a unilateral repudiation of the Black Sea clauses.

This Russian move constituted a breach of international law but it was completely successful. Bismarck would have preferred Gorchakov to have waited until the indignation of the European courts at Germany's victory had died down, but there was no alternative to supporting Russia. The Russian circular letter to the signatories of the Treaty of Paris and particularly the covering notes sent to individual governments showed Gorchakov's exceptionally clever penmanship. The circular letters were in the lofty tone of the great power, but the covering notes were perfectly attuned to the character of their recipients: for Bismarck 'a hearty handshake,' for London the calming assurance of Russia's wish to preserve the Ottoman Empire and the certainty that there would not be war; for Vienna a short and dry announcement with the acknowledgment of an earlier Austrian proposal; for Florence encouragement regarding Italy's claims to Rome; for Constantinople sweet reasonableness now that the only stumbling-block to better relations between the two states had been removed; for defeated France a particularly friendly note, accompanied by an oral promise from the Russian envoy of support for France at the peace conference. In mid-November Russia announced that if a meeting of a congress had been possible she would have placed the whole question before it because of its vital importance for her. The conference met after the event; in January and February 1871 the Black Sea Conference met in London and on 13 March 1871 gave international sanction to the Russian *fait accompli*.

The abrogation of the Black Sea clauses was only the beginning. For Russia the programme for a revision of the Treaty of Paris led on to the re-establishment of her predominance in the Balkans.

But the foundation of the German Empire rendered invalid all the political presuppositions on which Russia's Balkan policy, and indeed her position among the great powers, was based. As embodied in the personal policies of Alexander II Russia's attitude made the unification of Germany easier in three respects: by the neutralization of Austria, brought about by military threat; by the toleration of the annexation of Alsace-Lorraine and by waiving the demand for a congress – this last fitting in with Russia's own interests. There can be no doubt that this support – the only effective help given in Europe to the founding of the German Empire – was granted because the unification of Germany was seen to be a conservative, dynastic act, not a nationalistic, revolutionary one.

Germany was aware of her indebtedness: in a telegram to Alexander II on 2 March 1871 Emperor William expressed Prussia's realization that the localization of the war was due to the Russian emperor's attitude. The telegram was signed 'yours, with lifelong gratitude, William'. Yet the Germans, well disposed towards monarchy, underrated the importance of Russian public opinion at this time, which was wholeheartedly pro-French and anti-German. Bismarck knew, of course, that only Alexander II and a few of those closest to him supported Germany.

The following years showed that this benevolence – even if supported by the emperor's personal predilections – was not without political calculation. In September 1872, little more than eighteen months after the proclamation of the German Reich, Alexander II, by an unexpected and unwelcome appearance in Berlin, prevented the signing of a bilateral agreement between the Austrian and German emperors. The Berlin meeting of the three emperors, on the surface a brilliant demonstration of the concord reigning among the conservative powers, lost some of its glitter, however, with Gorchakov's assurance to France that the imperial powers would not unite against her. In the spring of 1873 Alexander II brought about the conclusion of a Russo-German military convention in St Petersburg which was, in effect, a bilateral defensive alliance. But the League of the Three Emperors, concluded that same year in Vienna – 'a direct and personal *entente* among sovereigns' – although it was only a consultative pact gave Bismarck the opportunity to regard the bilateral military agreement as void.

This league, which appeared to guarantee the existing order in Europe, was, however, rather brittle. Each of the three partners wanted something from the others, which was given only with the greatest reluctance: Russia, looking for support for her Balkan and Turkish policy, saw the German Reich as a guarantor for Austria-Hungary's loyalty; Austria-Hungary depended on Germany's future support in conferences which might have to deal with Russian pressure from the southeast while Germany was interested in obtaining the neutrality of the other two powers in case she might become involved in a new conflict with France.

But the Russian government was not prepared to forgo an improvement in Russo-French relations for the sake of an understanding with Germany, as was shown during the 'war-in-sight' crisis when Alexander II and Gorchakov seized the opportunity, presented to them by the mood of alarm which Bismarck had stirred up to discourage French rearmament, to complain to Berlin, soon after a similar intervention by the British envoy. Russia took credit for this step, representing it as a rescue operation on behalf of France. Admittedly the peace had not been in danger at any moment, but France believed – erroneously – that Russia had preserved her from a German preventive war. Contributory to this was the famous circular letter in which Gorchakov, after the Berlin discussions, sought to preserve the advantages gained by his *démarche*: dated 13 May 1875, this elegantly phrased dispatch announced that Alexander II had left Berlin completely convinced of the genuineness of the conciliatory intentions that prevailed there and which guaranteed the continuance of peace. But Bismarck's sharp eye read between the lines and saw Russia's attempt to appear as France's powerful protector. The Russians paid for their success for Bismarck bore a lasting resentment against their foreign minister.

In the succeeding years Russo-Prussian relations were to decline still further. Unrest in Herzegovina in July 1875 and the subsequent Serbian and Montenegrin revolt against the Turks caused Russian public opinion, carried along for the first time by a strong pan-Slavic sentiment, to demand that Russia should exercise her historic role as the defender of the Balkan Christians. But prevented by the provisions of the Treaty of Paris, which were still in force, Russia had to seek agreement from the other signatories before she could intervene. That the concept of 'Europe' should take central place in the language of Russian diplomacy during these years was only natural, and in keeping with treaty law; for the Russian Empire could act only as a mandatary. So as to avoid the mistakes made in the Crimean War Gorchakov first tried to win over Austria-Hungary. Partly successful in that, he turned to Germany. Hoping to draw on the reserves of gratitude owed by William I since 1871 and encouraged by the advances of a German emissary the Russians awaited an assurance from Bismarck that, should the necessity arise, Germany would keep Austria-Hungary in check – just as Russia had done in 1870. That Bismarck should want to avoid such a commitment is understandable. And it was in his interest at this time – just as it was with the abrogation of the Black Sea clauses – that Russia should have to act on her own without any support from the European powers. Even a weak German effort on Russia's behalf would have been of great value. In this way the paradoxical situation arose that while there were no more faithful Europeans than the Russians Bismarck mocked this 'shadow-boxing with Europeanism': 'I have always found the word Europe on the lips of those politicians who wanted something from other powers which they dared not demand in their own names.' That in various ways Bismarck encouraged the Russians to take unilateral action there can be no doubt, but he avoided giving concrete promises.

The war waged by the Russians against the Turks in 1877–78 and concluded with a decisive though hard-won victory was – as Gorchakov's colleague Jomini wrote – 'more a war of sentiment than of reason'. It was, without any doubt, a serious error of judgment on the part of the Russians – Gorchakov was lapsing into senility – to have taken much more from the Turks in the preliminary Peace of San Stefano (1878) than the next most interested powers were prepared to tolerate. In view of a British and Austro-Hungarian threat of war Russia saw that the only way out of the situation was the calling of a conference, even though this might lead to the abandonment of considerable gains. Giving way to a personal plea from Alexander II, Bismarck called together the Congress of Berlin, though not until he had laid down as a precondition of his participation that Russia should come to a preliminary settlement with her main opponents, Britain and Austria-Hungary. At the congress – over which he presided – he confined his mediation within the bounds of the arrangements already made, much to Russia's disappointment. Neither before nor now was it possible to activate German power on behalf of Russia's prestige in the Balkans. Russia had underrated the opposition and she was forced to drop her plans for the creation of a Greater Bulgaria. She felt that the advantages won at the congress were insignificant in comparison with the sacrifices of the war. More significantly, she believed that she had been insufficiently supported by

55 The Russo-Turkish War; Bulgarian villagers returning to their homes under Russian escort. Engraving from *The Illustrated London News*, 23 February 1878.

Germany. Certainly in 1879 she found herself in a state of isolation, but the increase in internal revolutionary activity within the empire – which will be discussed in the next chapter – pushed her into an *entente* with Germany, the strongest of the conservative military powers. Bismarck, who in 1879 concluded a secret defensive alliance with Austria-Hungary which was intended as a shield against Russian attack, was able to conclude the Three Emperors' Alliance in 1881, this time with reciprocal neutrality obligations.

Succeeding his murdered father in 1881 Alexander III continued the same policies and alliances. The Three Emperors' Alliance, which was renewed for a further three years in 1884, was adhered to despite very strong objections from Russian public opinion. 'For us it is essential', wrote the Russian foreign minister, Nikolai Giers, Gorchakov's successor, in the autumn of 1885, 'to maintain harmony among the three empires.' His strongest critic, the editor of the *Moskovskiya Vedomosti*, M. V. Katkov, wrote at the end of July 1886: 'our pilgrimages to Prince Bismarck remind us a little of the ancient journeys to the Golden Horde', i.e. the visits to pay tribute to the Tartar overlord. In the place of pan-Slavic wishful thinking there now emerged a Russian nationalism for which even Balkan politics were but a means to an end. Russia's claim to a decisive influence on Bulgaria was accepted by Germany, for Bismarck declined to support Bulgaria's incipient independence movement and he disclaimed any interest in Bulgarian affairs. The crisis in Anglo-Russian affairs on the issue of Russian expansion in Central Asia in 1885 was settled – as has been already mentioned – by a bilateral agreement.

The Three Emperors' Alliance was not renewed in 1887 but was replaced by a secret Russo-German neutrality pact (the so-called 'Reinsurance Treaty'). The 'very secret' additional clause, the promise of German 'diplomatic and moral support' for an active Russian policy in the Straits, was included in the treaty against the wishes of the Russian foreign minister Giers and his closest associate, the ex-head of chancellery, later foreign minister, Count Lamsdorf, but in agreement with the Russian ambassadors in Berlin. Bismarck's objective appears to have been the incitement of Alexander III towards policies of risk, just as Bismarck had done in 1870 and 1876, hoping to intensify opposition among Russia's neighbours and thereby to ease Germany's international position.

Despite this, soon after the conclusion of the Reinsurance Treaty Bismarck introduced measures designed to weaken Russia, but whose effect was to lead to a new orientation of Russian foreign policy. Following Bismarck's refusal to allow the German deposit banks to deal in Russian securities (10 November 1887) and the systematic discrediting of Russian loan securities in Germany, Russian loan policy and the Russian capital market shifted to France. Independently of this, political animosities developed during the period of the Russo-German treaty, corresponding closely to the attitude of the Russian and German public, while at the same time an inclination towards a political understanding gathered force both in Russia and France. Still, in 1890 when the Reinsurance Treaty came up for renewal, the Russian foreign ministry wanted a continuation of the contractual relationship with Germany, even without the Straits clause; for as Giers put it, at least something 'in writing would guarantee the preservation of the essential foundation of the relationship, independent of any change in personnel'.

After Bismarck's fall nobody in Berlin was willing to take up these suggestions, not because of any intention to arouse opposition against Russia but for fear that a contractual relationship with Russia might affect Germany's relationships with Austria-Hungary and Britain.

56 Above, the Giant Battery before Plevna. Engraving from Cassell's *History of the Russo–Turkish War, 1877–79.*

57 Congress at the Radziwill Palace, Berlin. Disraeli and Gorchakov in conclave with the Turkish minister. Engraving from *The Illustrated London News*, 29 June 1878.

A cautious *rapprochement* between the Russian Empire and a revitalized French Republic led – in 1892 – to a military convention between the two powers which had all the trappings of an alliance. This was a change of course in Russian foreign policy. But the Franco-Russian alliance was not the result of any single political event, neither the anti-Russian German credit policy nor the failure to renew the Reinsurance Treaty nor the appearance of a pro-British trend in German policy. It was, rather, a new attempt on the part of Russia to strengthen her position in Europe more easily than she had been able to do by following the old-fashioned policy of monarchical solidarity. Now she could take advantage of the strained relations following the growing dynamic of the imperialistic interests of all the great powers.

Russia's involvement in the tensions of world politics was not so much the result of friction in Europe, e.g. rivalry in the Balkans or her special disputes with Germany. Primarily it was due to the changes which occurred in the Far East. One turning-point was the Treaty of Shimonoseki (April 1895), which ended the Sino-Japanese War with a dramatic increase in Japan's power, in itself a serious danger to Russian interests. As the Liaotung peninsula with the harbour of Port Arthur was to pass to the Japanese, Russian plans for Manchuria were now endangered. Russia succeeded in winning round her former ally Germany and her current ally France to a joint intervention in favour of China which forced Japan to submit to the pressure of the three powers (November 1895).

By supporting Russia in the Far East the German emperor, William II, hoped to divert her attention from Europe and to weaken her alliance with France. But his conception of the Russian leadership was quite unreal: he had never met his cousin, the emperor; he was unaware of the strong tradition of power in the Russian foreign ministry and the importance of financial interests was beyond his understanding. Thus the allegorical painting which William II commissioned and dedicated to the Russian emperor in the summer of 1895 was worthless as a work of art, ineffective as a piece of propaganda and painfully unsuitable as a romantic interpretation of Russia's functions in Asia. The painting carried the inscription: 'Peoples of Europe, guard your most sacred possessions!' It showed – according to William II – the European powers, each represented by a kind of national genius, called together by the Archangel Michael to unite

58 Alexander III seated on the right, with members of the English aristocracy.

59 Nicholas II visits Napoleon's tomb at the Invalides in Paris.

under the Cross in resisting the encroachments of Buddhism, paganism and barbarism. Russia's imperialistic policies in the Far East had as little to do with the Cross as those of any other European power. Her total immunity to an artificial 'Europa' ideology, as offered to her, can be said to demonstrate how Russia's governing class had become completely integrated into its corresponding milieu in contemporary Europe, needing neither a dramatic role nor picturesque costumes to identify itself as European.

In their unscrupulousness the methods employed by Russia in extending her power in Asia differed not at all from those of the other colonial powers. The secret treaty signed in Moscow on 3 June 1896 with the Chinese chancellor (who received a bribe of three million roubles) gave Russia permission to extend the Trans-Siberian Railway across Manchuria, i.e. through Chinese territory. In addition each side promised assistance to the other in the case of Japanese aggression against either themselves or Korea.

Six days later Russia and Japan agreed – in another secret agreement, also signed in Moscow – to a condominium in Korea, without any demarcation of spheres of influence. This gave the Russians an opportunity for decisive influence at the Korean court and to break into the economy of the country through private concessions. But barely two years later the Russian government recognized the primacy of Japanese economic interests in Korea (Rosen-Nishi Agreement, Tokyo, April 1898).

Shortly before this, in March 1898, Russia forced China, through an ultimatum and bribery, to lease the southern part of the Liaotung peninsula. This was prompted by fear of a British counter-measure to the recent seizure of Kiao-chow by Germany. By the end of March the Russians were in occupation of Port Arthur. This made nonsense of the Russo-Chinese treaty concluded two years previously in Moscow. The chain-reaction begun by the German occupation of Kiao-chow ended in the British leasing of Wei-hai-wei in April 1898.

In consideration of Russia's sensational expansionist policy in the Far East it is not surprising that the Russian government, presenting a scheme of an entirely different kind, was suspected of being hypocritical. But Nicholas II's proposal, formalized by Count Muraviev, for the calling of an international conference on the suspension of armament and the humanizing of warfare, was taken seriously by the powers. On the invitation of Queen Wilhelmina of the Netherlands, all the European states and the United States, Mexico, China, Japan and Siam sent representatives to the Hague, where the first conference opened in May 1899.

The Russians, who had planned the first agenda for the conference, were suspected of aiming at a general curb in armaments chiefly because of their own financial difficulties and as a smokescreen for their own imperialistic policies. The proposal was either – as with William II – mockingly dismissed as a piece of humanitarian humbug on the part of the young emperor or taken up unenthusiastically and suspiciously as a more or less clever attempt to mystify the public. The British, French and German representatives rejected the Russian proposal from similar motives, although within the conference their tactics varied according to their different approaches to public opinion. The results of the First and Second Hague Peace Conferences cannot be discussed here; today they appear relevant to everybody.

Various motives can be discerned behind the initiative of the Russian government: undoubtedly financial considerations played a part, considering the additional burden placed on the exchequer by the necessary modernization of Russian arms, but at the same time questions of prestige also played their part, as well as the desire to appease the powers by a demonstration of peaceful intentions – this last on the advice of the head of the Asiatic department in the foreign ministry. Finally there was the emperor's genuine concern over the increasing destructive power of modern weaponry. This humanitarian motive, based ultimately on religious grounds, cannot be dismissed because of the tactical and political arguments.

By 1898 the Russians, by their unsystematic, aggressive and illusory policy in the Far East, had manœuvered themselves into a very unfavourable position, further aggravated by the Boxer Rebellion in the summer of 1900. The paralysation of their railway in Manchuria by the rebels forced them to mobilize. But the ensuing occupation of Manchuria by the Russians, the apparent rounding off of their East Asian imperium, was not without its dangers, and they were well advised to evacuate Manchuria in 1902, in agreement with China. But no attempt had been made to come to terms with Japan, arrogantly underestimated in Russian governing circles. A mixture of false information and the growing importance of private capitalistic interests led to a wrong assessment of the situation, while in St Petersburg an old-fashioned European sense of superiority drowned the warning voices. Unwilling to withdraw from Korea and – this was the decisive difference – unwilling to make allowances for Japanese interests in Manchuria the Russian Empire, so backward in many ways, slid into war with the modernized East Asian Imperial power which since 1902 had been allied with Britain.

The Russo-Japanese War, although waged thousands of miles away, had an intense effect on the European political world, Russian involvement making it in some respects a European event. After a surprise lightning attack on Port Arthur (February 1904) where the Russian fleet was at anchor, masses of Japanese troops were able to land in Korea largely unhindered. Surrounded by Japanese, resistance broken, Port Arthur was forced to capitulate (January 1905) after unbelievably bloody assaults and titanic efforts at relief. In one of those romantic gestures beloved of William II he awarded both the Japanese commander Nogi and the Russian defender Stössel Germany's highest war decoration. But as the fortress could have held out for another fortnight – as was afterwards proved – Stössel was court-martialled and condemned to death, though, after his sentence had been commuted to confinement in a fortress, he was reprieved. The moving up of Russian supplies along the single-track, over-extended Trans-Siberian Railway needed plenty of time. The battle of Mukden (March 1905) was, as far as the number of combatants on both sides was concerned, the greatest battle in history to that date. It ended in a Japanese victory, though it was not decisive enough to bring about a military surrender. Even the destruction of the Russian Baltic fleet near the Tsushima Islands (May 1905) did not make the Russian position hopeless.

The naval catastrophe in the Tsushima Straits aroused the interest of the world largely because the months-long journey of the Baltic fleet – coaled by the Hamburg-Amerika Line – around the Cape of Good Hope and across the Indian Ocean had attracted enormous publicity, increased by the Dogger Bank affair (October 1904) in which Russian warships had fired on British fishing-boats, under the impression that they were Japanese torpedo-boats. The destruction of the Baltic fleet exposed the backwardness of Russia's naval armaments, but Russia's land forces were in no way exhausted. At any rate the war was most unpopular in Russia, primarily because of the internal tensions and the attempts to solve them by revolution. On the other hand Japan was pushed to the limit of her financial and military capacity by the war. However, the end of Russian expansion in the Far East seemed imminent after the Peace of Portsmouth (New Hampshire) in September 1905, which was arranged through the mediation of President Theodore Roosevelt. Russia withdrew from Korea and Manchuria and ceded Port Arthur and southern Sakhalin to the Japanese. But it was not the collapse of the Russian position in the Far East, nor was it within logic that such a defeat could inactivate Russia in Asia.

It is curious how little effect the Russo-Japanese War had on the European consciousness. It should have had some: never before had the destructiveness of modern warfare displayed itself so nakedly, neither in the Franco-Prussian War of 1870–71 nor in the Russo-Turkish War of 1877–78; neither in the Spanish-American War of 1898 nor in the Boer War of 1899–1902. Never before had such vast armies confronted one another nor had mechanical fire-power been deployed with such deadly effect. In a way the Russian initiative, which resulted in the first Peace Conference, led to a new evaluation of the disasters of war. Nevertheless the Russian leadership continued the traditional policy of rearmament and thereby increasing the risk of war, just as all the other European powers did. Was Russia too European in this respect or not European enough? Such reflections reveal the flaw of this 'European' categorization in the evaluation of these developments. Had not Japan 'Europeanized' herself faster and more efficiently? Or was Russia more 'European' because she was more old-fashioned?

An intelligent observer of Imperial Russia's foreign policy, Baron Boris Nolde, at one time a department director in the Russian foreign ministry, once made the remark that Imperial Russia could always choose between various goals and could change direction from one day to the next, thus giving her policy the character 'of a free play of thoughts, often improvised'.

Admittedly, the still-born treaty which William II inveigled Nicholas II into signing during their meeting among the rocky islands of the Gulf of Finland near Björköe in July 1905 did not belong to this 'free play of thoughts'. In an exchange of views preceding the informal signing of this 'defensive alliance' William II was told that Russia did not wish to conclude the treaty without France's participation in the preliminaries. When Nicholas II then agreed to sign the treaty on the understanding that France would be invited to accede to it only when it had come into force, his signature was binding, despite the fact that it lacked the approval of the Russian foreign minister. But taking the context into consideration the treaty was worthless. Although a French refusal was not allowed for in the text of the agreement it was easy to see, from Russia's wish to include France in any continental alliance, that she would not tolerate her reciprocal assistance pact with Germany being directed against France. In this sense Nicholas II informed his ally in November 1905 after France's deprecatory attitude. After this the Russians regarded the treaty as non-existent.

Russia's need of loans after the financial blood-letting of the Japanese War swung her round to France's side politically. In the first Morocco crisis of 1905–6 Russia was uninterested in the material differences separating France and Germany. German diplomacy did not see that for Russia there was no possibility of being neutral during the Algeciras Conference and so the unexpected Russian attitude was attributed to a supposed Russian national failing, ingratitude and arrogance. Baron von Schoen, later an ambassador, wrote to the German chancellor in March 1906 – causing William II to annotate busily – that Germany's 'loyal and high-minded attitude was difficult to comprehend for people of a low cultural level'. Such a point of view, mawkish, arrogant and determined to be resentful left little hope for an objective assessment of the prospects of either side. On the understanding that Russian policy favoured France, the raising of a loan of 2,000 million francs in Paris was approved. Russia's wish that Germany should participate so as to give the loan an international character, was not acceded to in Berlin.

The Russian foreign minister, Count Muraviev, in a conversation with the German ambassador, Prince Radolin, in St Petersburg in June 1899, pointed out that it was an illusion to believe that Britain was an irreconcilable enemy of Russia. It was, he went on, possible for Russia to come to an understanding with Britain over their differences in Central Asia. On the German side this met not only with scepticism but also, judging from William II's marginal notes, with indignation, being regarded as a coarse attempt at deception. Yet eighteen months later Radolin asserted that an Anglo-Russian *rapprochement* was imminent. However, Russia's imprudence in the Far East interrupted these efforts at agreement and led temporarily

to new tensions. But the conclusion of the *Entente Cordiale* in 1904, generally accepted in Russia, was greeted with enthusiasm. Count Lamsdorf, Russian foreign minister after Muraviev, was an advocate of a settlement with Britain while his successor Alexander Izvolsky (from May 1906) made it one of his main tasks to conclude a treaty with Britain. The negotiations which began in June 1906 led to the St Petersburg agreement of 31 August 1907. Although this was concerned with the demarcation of spheres of influence in Persia, a convention about Afghanistan and an arrangement about Tibet it went far beyond the material interests of the agreement and brought about an understanding between the signatories. The new relationship was given expression in the meeting between Nicholas II and Edward VII in Reval in June 1908. Izvolsky believed that he had made concessions to British interests in Central Asia and had, therefore, won Britain's support for Russian interests in Europe.

On the conclusion of her *entente* with Britain Russia turned to her Balkan and Straits policies. Her disputes with Austria-Hungary were settled in two agreements in 1897 and 1903. Now as Izvolsky developed new plans Austria-Hungary met him with concrete proposals. The Congress of Berlin (1878) gave the Danube Monarchy the right to administer Bosnia and Herzegovina, which right it now wanted to convert into outright annexation so as to block any claim to sovereignty by the sultan. Such an act appeared to be possible without the consent of the other signatories of the Congress of Berlin provided that Russia, the power most interested in the area, gave her consent. Izvolsky, confident of Britain's agreement, was prepared to do this if, on her side, Austria-Hungary raised no objection to Russia receiving the right of free passage through the Straits for her warships. An agreement between the two foreign ministers, Izvolsky and Count Alois von Aehrenthal, was reached in September 1908 at Buchlau, the Moravian estate of Count Berchtold, then ambassador to Russia. But this agreement, a success for Austria-Hungary, proved to be a heavy defeat for Russia. Vienna announced the annexation of Bosnia and Herzegovina, as agreed, but Izvolsky after meeting with difficulties in Paris on the issue of the Straits settlement encountered open opposition to it in London. In contrast to this Austria-Hungary succeeded in obtaining the approval of all the powers for her action, except that of Russia, for Izvolsky now wanted an international conference to tackle the issue. Serbia, relying on Russian support, mobilized her troops against Austria-Hungary. But as at that time a war was out of the question for Russia, Izvolsky had no option but to give in, especially when Germany, identifying herself publicly with Austria-Hungary, demanded – in a peremptory fashion – a decision. Although this near-ultimatum did not threaten war its phraseology was menacing: unless Russia backed down Germany would 'let things take their course'; i.e. she would not stand in the way if Austria-Hungary decided to 'settle' matters with Serbia. This was a very unfriendly attitude on the part of Germany, showing complete indifference to Russia's inevitable diplomatic defeat.

The German near-ultimatum, conveyed through the ambassador at St Petersburg, was not drawn up by the chancellor himself but by Kiderlen-Wächter, later secretary of state, who, it was reported, had remarked to a Rumanian that he knew that the Russians did not want war and that he intended to profit from this. 'I wanted to demonstrate that the period of Russia's tutelage over Germany, which dates back to 1815, has passed for ever.' If the frame of mind which led to this kind of talk has been interpreted correctly this was a policy of resentment, i.e. bad policy. It was no better than Russia's poorly prepared tactics on the question of the Straits clauses and the reckless, singleminded pursuit of her own interests by the Danube Monarchy.

In Russia hostility to Germany gained more and more support. In the summer of 1908 a German diplomat in St Petersburg reported the 'hatred of Germans in the inmost being of all politically minded or even sentient Russians'. In the printed arrangements for the Russian military manœuvres of August 1910 one of the two sides was explicitly called the 'German' force instead of being given an abstract label according to international practice. The Russian foreign minister, of course, expressed his regret for this tactless error, but during those years before 1914 Russo-German relations lacked mutual trust. The Potsdam Convention of 1910 by which Russia and Germany came to an agreement regarding their economic interests in the Orient brought no general change in relations.

Relations between St Petersburg and Vienna took a somewhat similar course. Russia counted on changes occurring in the Balkans and kept in view the ultimate goal, the extension of Russian sovereignty over the Straits. Not that this was necessary for the smooth operation of southern Russia's exports. Sazonov, Russian foreign minister from 1910, in a report to Nicholas II in November 1913 described the current state of the Straits question as 'in essence quite satisfactory'. But should the issue become activated Russia could not remain a spectator. Although sovereignty over the Bosporus was incorporated in Russian plans, admittedly only as a distant goal, responsible department heads understood that this could be achieved only by a general European war. This is not to say that Russia was actively preparing for such a war, but should one come her aims were not just defensive in character.

The Russians had no easy task in their dealings with the peoples of the Balkans, who were not prepared to subordinate themselves implicitly to Russian interests or even to co-ordinate their own interests with those of Russia. Serbia's expansionist plans, which could only be realized at the expense of the Danubian Monarchy, were encouraged by Russia's envoy at Belgrade but Serbia's demands for a harbour on the Adriatic, after the victorious Balkan War of 1912, were not supported by St Petersburg. Inevitably Russia's advice to Belgrade to drop the proposal – given mainly because of France's reserved attitude – was interpreted as a sign of weakness. Neither Sazonov himself nor Baron Schilling, his head of chancellery, were pan-Slavs: the aristocratic ruling circles regarded themselves as a cut above Balkan nationalists. At the same time they could not afford to allow the Serbs and Bulgars to develop resentment or disappointment in case this might be exploited by Austrians and Germans, raising the spectre of a blocking of the Straits.

This is pertinent to Russia's attitude in the July 1914 crisis. At the very earliest opportunity and with perfect clarity the Russian foreign ministry explained that Russia would not tolerate a weakening or humiliation of Serbia (so Schilling told the Italian ambassador on 16 July). Subsequently the foreign minister informed the German ambassador Count Pourtalès on 24 July that on no account would Russia accept a localization of the conflict. When Sazonov, an intelligent and highly civilized diplomatist, displayed an 'ineradicable hatred' for Austria-Hungary it would seem that he deliberately raised the emotional temperature so as to stake out for the German ambassador the limits to Russia's readiness to negotiate. This is substantiated by Alexander Krivoshein, the minister of agriculture, who enjoyed a special position of authority in the cabinet. According to the unpublished notes of the minister of finance, P. L. Bark, Krivoshein told the council of ministers on 24 July that 'Nobody in Russia wants war. The disastrous effects of the recent armed conflict with Japan showed the grave risks which Russia would run in a similar situation.' But war could break out, despite all concessions. It was up to the council of ministers to decide which course offered the least risk. It was his opinion 'that stiffer language on our part was alone capable of curbing the unreasonableness of the Central Powers'. This view was shared by the minister of finance, as little a chauvinist as his colleague.

The course of events is clear. Serbia's answer to Austria-Hungary's ultimatum was regarded as unsatisfactory in Vienna. Sazonov tried to internationalize this decision by searching for a compromise formula which would allow Austria-Hungary to save face while preventing Serbia from being humiliated, though he did not preclude the possibility that Serbia would have to be taught a lesson. Only from 29 July onwards did the views of the military establishment gain the upper hand, mainly because partial mobilization directed against Austria-Hungary, which did not make a general war unavoidable, could only be changed into general mobilization with great difficulty and delay because of the poor state of preparedness of Russia's technical and organizational machine. When hope of a political solution of the conflict faded Sazonov extracted from the emperor the command for general mobilization on the afternoon of 30 July. Nicholas II also knew that this meant war and he took the decision with the greatest reluctance.

Outside observers later assumed that a 'war party', intimately connected with the court and having the Grand Prince Nikolai Nikolaevich at its head, had pushed the weak-willed emperor into war. It was presumed that internal political considerations had played a decisive part, particularly the argument that mobilization and the state of emergency would help to neutralize revolutionary tendencies. In fact awareness of the danger of revolution had been used as an argument against war as well as for it. These motives did not play a decisive part. Certainly there were groups of warmongers but the decisions reached by the foreign minister and the emperor, who took sole responsibility, were not influenced either by emotion or sabre-rattling. The logic of prestige politics and power politics prevailed, and in some respects it was also old-fashioned and perhaps 'too European'. If Imperial Russia's governing classes had been more aware of the possibilities for development in their own Eurasian world perhaps they would not have taken the loss of prestige in the Balkans so badly, provided of course that they had been able to find ways and means to safeguard the vital corn exports via the Black Sea and the Straits. But who was to know how long the war was to last? Everyone was as astonished by the length of the war as by the extent of the changes caused by it. For the last time Russia shared the opportunities and the illusions, the misery and the pride, the community of interests and the intimate hostility of the *Concert Européen*, before a new era dawned.

When Turkey entered the war on the side of the Central Powers in the late autumn of 1914 the Russian foreign ministry took out the contingency plans which had been drawn up before the war for just this eventuality. The Allies agreed to what had always been previously refused, Russia's acquisition of Constantinople and the Straits. The secret agreement made by Sazonov in March 1915 through the exchange of memoranda with Britain and France contained a carefully restricted promise. An *aide-mémoire* of the British embassy in

Petrograd, dated 12 March 1915, stated that: 'Subject to the war being carried on and brought to a successful conclusion, and to the desiderata of Great Britain and France in the Ottoman Empire and elsewhere being realized. . . . His Majesty's Government will agree to the Russian Government's *aide-mémoire* relative to Constantinople and the Straits, the text of which was communicated . . . on February 19th/ March 4th instant.' That meant that Constantinople, the west side of the Bosporus, the Sea of Marmora and the Dardanelles were to be incorporated in the Russian Empire. But the agreement remained purely hypothetical as the Russians were unable to take part in the Gallipoli campaign in 1915. The publication of the Straits Agreement in the autumn of 1916, insisted upon by the Russian government for internal reasons, had no effect, the disorder in the empire killing all interest in distant war aims. By this time the historical romanticism of an alleged national duty had lost its sheen.

Already during the first year of the war it was apparent that Russia, technically backward, especially in the field of transportation, was not capable of waging a long war with an enemy highly qualified both in military and technical matters. Yet Emperor Nicholas II, who alone could make the decision, did not contemplate the possibility of a separate peace with the Central Powers. Not only was this because the London Agreement of 5 September 1914 made it impossible for Britain, France or Russia to negotiate a separate peace but because

61 A Russian army was routed by the Germans at Tannenberg in August 1914 and over 100,000 prisoners taken.

62 Russian army in retreat.

he felt in conscience bound to keep the oath he had sworn at the outbreak of the war, and he felt a personal solidarity with the army,
especially since he took over the supreme command in September
1915. It is well known that after the February revolution of 1917 the
Provisional Government also refused a separate peace, although with
the entry into the war of the United States it would hardly have meant
the end of the war.

Of all the Allies, Russia suffered the heaviest defeats and with 1·7
million people dead and almost 5 million wounded endured the
greatest loss of life. One of the most important reasons, even the
decisive reason, why the Provisional Government failed to preserve
the freedom which it had won in March 1917 was the impossibility of
withdrawing this unhappy country from the war, so deep was her
involvement with Europe's destiny. Old Russia perished because she
was too European.

VI AN OPEN EUROPE

Russia's defeat in the Crimean War was followed by a 'new era' of fundamental reforms of which the most important legislative act was the abolition of serfdom by Alexander II's Manifesto of 3 March 1861.

The emancipation of the peasants was long overdue. As already mentioned, it had been carried out in the Baltic provinces in 1816–19, but as far as the rest of Russia was concerned it was to get no further than the emperor's agenda throughout the reign of Nicholas I. Then barely two weeks after the conclusion of the Treaty of Paris Alexander II announced in Moscow his intention to abolish the 'ownership of souls'. No longer was it a question of 'if' but of 'how'. The first preparatory committee, called together by the emperor, met in January 1857. The unfortunate consequences of emancipation in Livonia, Estonia and Courland left no room for doubt that personal freedom alone, without the additional legal security of the peasant's right to arable land, would have harmful effects. Towards the end of 1857 the emperor laid down the basic principle of the reform: personal emancipation was to go hand in hand with the allocation of land. A further principle dealt with the problem of compensation for the landlords: the landlord was to be compensated only for the land withdrawn from his use, not for the liberated serfs. Yet there remained ample room for the advocacy of the landlords' interests within the confines of these principles. The end result of four years of deliberations by various committees at different levels was a law which certainly did away with the deepest social and legal distinction between Russia and the rest of Europe. While a peasant population of about 47 millions became legally free, in two respects the measure had serious and momentous defects.

Land which until this date had been tilled by peasants and owned by landlords now passed, by purchase, into the possession of the peasant communes which allotted the land to the individual peasant. This was not a permanent allocation, the land being subject to periodic redistribution. By linking the law to the institution of the *mir* it was hoped to safeguard every peasant's claim to the use of land. A two-thirds majority was necessary in a meeting of the commune before such redistribution could be abandoned, while a similar majority was necessary for the exclusion of an individual parcel of land for conversion into private property. The commitment to communal ownership was a mistake, for the proposed collectives were much too small in extent and took no account of the possibility of a natural increase in the population. The doubling of the peasant population in the succeeding decades burst through the available land allotments. But apart from this there were maximum and minimum norms, which varied from region to region. The minimum was not enough to support a family and in some cases was even smaller than in the pre-reform period. Very quickly differentiation took place, the economically stronger peasants becoming wealthy by buying and leasing land while weaker peasants sank into destitution. Dependence on supplementary earnings from agricultural labouring, rural handicrafts and factory work became characteristic of the peasant. In addition to land hunger the redemption annuity, which was high in comparison to the value of the land, was one of the flaws in the emancipation edict. The regulation of these redemption annuities was undertaken by the State, which compensated the landlords for their loss through the issue of securities.

These agrarian reforms affected the whole of Russia's political, economic and social life. The disappointment of the peasants expressed itself in new disturbances, and the agrarian problem was to remain the central problem of Russian internal politics. This was so not only because about 80 per cent of the population lived from the land up to the revolution but because the complete adaptation of Russia's economy to modern governmental and social requirements was, in the first place, an agro-political problem. How slowly Russia's urbanization proceeded can be seen from these figures: the urban population of Russia rose from 9·6 per cent (1867) to 11·7 per cent (1897) and 13·3 per cent (1914). In comparison with this France had an urban population of 40 per cent, Germany 54 per cent and England almost 80 per cent around 1900.

Any Russian government which set before itself the task of overcoming the country's material backwardness so as to make it capable of competing with Europe and to ensure its independence had to start from the premise that everything depended on a 'correct' agrarian economy. It was neither enough to raise the peasant's

63 *On the road. Death of a settler.* Painting by S. Ivanov, 1889. Tretyakov Gallery.

standard of living – necessary as that was – by the development.of cottage industries nor to extend peasant landholdings through the provision of easier credits for land purchase. The Peasants' Land Bank (1883) was founded for this purpose with the result that one-third of the land left to the landlords in 1861 had passed to the peasants by 1905. Even more important was the fact that agriculture which produced more than half the income of the State had the greatest possible economic effect, by making possible an increase in capital through its exporting capacity. This in Russia led to the home production of necessities leaving the State less dependent on capital-consuming imports or foreign investments. Highly taxed consumer goods also served the purpose of capital growth. 'If Russia had had central-European norms of consumption she would not have been in a position to export foodstuffs' (Nötzold). Russian sugar was cheaper in London than in Russia, while in 1913 Russia was – even more so than Canada – the world's foremost supplier of wheat. Yet in 1913 not only was it necessary to import farming machinery into Russia but scythes, ploughs and harrows as well.

Russian industrialization which took on an 'American' tempo only from the end of the nineteenth century, needed State regulation just as much as agriculture. Without personalizing these issues the name of Sergei Julievich Witte, minister of finance and, for a short period, prime minister, must be mentioned; for he, with his modern approach and his exceptional energy, played a leading part in Russian economic policy. He introduced the tariff system which from the 1890s until the outbreak of the war was the necessary pre-condition for the rise of central industrial production: the growth and manufacture of cotton developed so rapidly that Russia's exports to China and Persia in 1913 exceeded those of England's, in the smelting and metallurgical industries, in coal-mining and in the production of crude oil. One of the characteristics of Russian industrialization was the small number of industrial areas, e.g. Moscow, St Petersburg, southern Ukraine. Another was the over-population of other regions that were without industries. The result was the clustering of factory workers in some central regions. Russia's factory workers more than doubled in the years between 1890 and 1912, yet they were only 2·4 per cent of the total population which was still four-fifths rural. From a sociological point of view the Russian working class was of peasant origin – so different from Germany where workers came from the

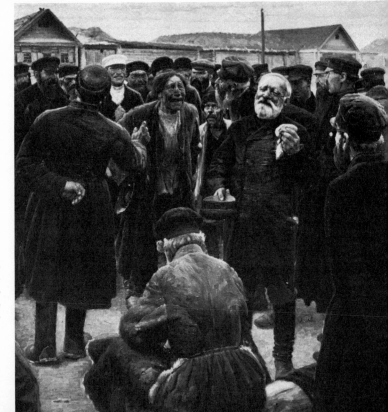

64 Meeting of the *mir*, the village commune. Painting by S. Korovin, 1893. Tretyakov Gallery, Moscow.

ranks of the artisans – and they retained their peasant characteristics. One difference, however, was that among factory workers the percentage of literates was twice that of the population as a whole. The protection of labour was in its infancy up to 1914.

The picture of the Russian economy up to the revolution presents some very sharp contrasts: side by side with pre-capitalistic characteristics throughout a large part of agriculture there were forms of early capitalism especially in the field of wages, working and living conditions in industrial towns and there were advanced capitalistic traits in heavy industry with its strong tendency towards monopolies. Among the worst drawbacks were the famines which recurred every few years in some of the agrarian regions. Despite the growth of industrial production and the development of its own capital market pre-revolutionary Russia needed foreign capital. In the original capital of Russian limited companies the share of foreign capital rose from 25 per cent in 1895 to 42 per cent in 1913. Loans from foreign governments were disproportionately high, yet it would not be true to say that financial policy was unsound. Investments were renumerative as well as productive. This was especially so in the building of the railways which, for the most part, were financed from abroad. But here interests other than economic also played their part; for France the role of banker had a strategic advantage and in Russia the bureaucracy and the military saw the function of the railways from conflicting viewpoints. Yet the railway network in 1914 was totally inadequate for strategic needs, in spite of the doubling of the track during the previous twenty years.

The radical agrarian reforms which Peter Stolypin, the last distinguished statesman of the imperial era, prime minister 1906–11, introduced, must be seen against the background of a whole range of economic and political problems. The simple basic idea of the reform carried out from 1906 was the conversion of peasant land into the private holdings of heads of families and the substitution of consolidated holdings for separate strips as well as the dissolution of the *mir* in favour of the economic activity of a peasantry marketing its own produce. Naturally this produced a sharp economic differentiation among the peasants, the strong growing stronger while the weak became weaker. By 1916 more than two million individual farms had been established and about one-fifth of the entire land under peasant occupation had been converted to private farms.

Before the revolution there were sharp differences of opinion as to whether communal property should be abolished or preserved. Stolypin as an upholder of the power of the State expected from this reorganization the stabilization of social conditions and the laying of a conservative foundation for the State while the social-democratic revolutionaries saw in the swing to a property-owning peasantry a revolutionary factor.

The social changes which were put in train from the 1860s brought a new Russia into being. One of the most effective means by which social forces were set free was the *Zemstvo* law of January 1864. This established local government on a broad basis: the rural gentry, the townspeople and the peasant communes sent representatives to the district assemblies which in turn selected the members of the provincial assemblies. District and provincial assemblies elected administrative bodies. The *Zemstvo* boards were given the right to impose by-laws, levy taxes, grant loans and petition although those powers were circumscribed. The new *Zemstvo* law of 1890 while assuring the aristocracy of a majority voice also increased State control. However, the principal of social self-government was already so strongly established than an area of public independence developed which contemporaries saw as in some ways 'a preparatory training for parliamentary government' (1898).

The high revenues from *Zemstvo* taxation (254 million roubles in 1913) made it possible for local government to engage in a whole range of activities, among which education and public health absorbed more than half of all income. But road programmes, agricultural improvements and social welfare were also well to the fore. Much loss of time was incurred, of course, battling against prejudice, mistrust and the dead hand of the old bureaucracy, and many battles were lost. But the building of schools, libraries and reading rooms, hospitals and mental homes, the appointment of doctors and midwives, veterinarians, agronomists and statisticians, the installation of telephones, the organization of cottage industries and many other services raised the whole world of public services to a new plane in Russian life. Administrative costs remained surprisingly low (6·8 per cent in 1913). Setting the pace in ensuring the functioning of the *Zemstva* was the local aristocracy, often belonging to the oldest families. Working with them, and of growing importance, were the professional classes, the so-called 'third element' which contributed

133

much to the democratization of the *Zemstvo* system. Among these public-spirited groups a new type developed, positive in approach and of great social importance, the *obshchestvenny deyatel'*, an untranslatable term for one active in the service of society without the expectation of material rewards.

During the 1890s a noticeable change took place in the awareness of the Russian public; the famine of 1891, the immediate result of an extremely poor harvest, unleashed so much social activity that a new era seemed to be dawning. At this time the so-called *beseda* circles developed, remaining in existence until 1905. They were discussion groups which brought together on a personal basis members of different political persuasion, all of them co-workers in local government, to discuss questions of public interest. Already, from the last years of Alexander II's reign constitutional reform was in the air. Only the emperor's assassination in 1881 prevented the appointment of an advisory representative body but the hopes turned towards the new emperor in the 1890s were to be dashed.

Apart from the emancipation of the serfs and the introduction of local government there were other reforms in the 1860s which had social and historical consequences. The army reform of 1874 brought in conscription and paved the way for the democratization of the officer corps; reforms in the system of justice, partly influenced by French pattern, led to the introduction of the jury system, the opening of legal proceedings to the public, the creation of justices of the peace and the organization of a legal profession. Finally there were municipal reforms which, on the basis of the Prussian three-class voting system, introduced municipal government on the basis of the census.

It may be asked what contributed most to making 'the fluidity of the Russian social structure' (A. Meyendorff) the most important characteristic of Russia's internal history. As a process it worked at different strata and at various speeds. Changes in production techniques, industrialization and capitalism brought rapid changes in some areas and to some social classes, while other areas of life and other classes remained unusually long in their archaic state.

A strong lever on Russian society and an active interpreter of its evolution was that small but effective class, the intelligentsia, in itself an expression of the unavoidable dissolution of Russia's old social two-class system. Its origins go back into the eighteenth century, its social base the enlightened aristocracy and the numerous *raznochintsy*,

65 Porcelain group of three Moscow coachmen made at the Gardner Factory, Moscow, c. 1890, which shows the new interest in local affairs engendered by the rise of nationalistic feeling after the 1850s.

'men of various ranks', who were difficult to classify but who ranged over the whole intellectual world. Rosa Luxemburg rightly observed (in 1904) that the Russian intelligentsia was much more *déclassé* than similar groups in Western Europe. The existence of such a class, detached from the social class structure, oriented towards Western European ideas, teaching, studying, writing and speaking, was contrary to the traditional social order and the existing regime whether they were reformers or revolutionaries. Their prestige derived from the high social regard which Russians pay to all intellectual work. Their strongest effect sprang from the fact that many of them had the power and magic of artistic expression, which ensured that literature in Russia was an evolutionary, disquieting force not just the reflection of a stagnant, complacent society.

There is hardly anything which shows so well Russia's similarity to the rest of Europe as the simultaneous rise of nationalism to a position of dominance. The dreamy national romanticism as much as the intolerant exclusiveness of national languages, the hubris of messianic

135

fervour as well as deep hatred and contempt for foreigners were common in Europe in the nineteenth and twentieth centuries.

The first signs of this new ideology appeared during the Wars of Liberation, then among the Decembrists, later as official policy in the reign of Nicholas I and among the Slavophiles. Nationalism in Russia rose to be the reigning social mood after the Polish rebellion of 1863. Herzen, who had until then surreptitiously influenced Russian public opinion through his London-based periodical *Kolokol* (The Bell), lost five-sixths of his readership in Russia when he sided with the Poles. The new spokesman for Russian public opinion was the former professor of philosophy M. N. Katkov with his great newspaper *Moskovskiya Vedomosti*. For almost the next quarter of a century, until his death in 1887, Katkov championed nationalistic demands in both internal and external political affairs.

From 1864 onwards, Russia's nationalistic politicians turned their eyes from Poland and Lithuania towards the empire's three non-Russian provinces along the Baltic. Livonia, Estonia and Courland were governed under their own laws and enjoyed an old-fashioned representative autonomy, in many ways like English local government. The class rights accorded the German landowning aristocracy and the municipal corporations in the towns gave them a leading role in public life. The Church was Lutheran and trilingual, the University of Dorpat and the entire grammar school system were German-speaking, as was the daily press, the book trade, the theatre and cultured society. German was not only the *lingua franca* of the provincial and municipal authorities but was predominantly that of the state authorities as well. To those whose thinking was dominated by the concept of a unitary national state the special legal and cultural situation in the Baltic provinces was anomalous.

When fears arose that the Estonians and Letts might be drawn towards the German element, with the consequent danger of a 'Baltic Finland' developing, opposition became vocal. Fuel was added to it through the obvious attraction which nationalistic tendencies in Germany had for the Baltic Germans. For years fierce wordy battles were waged between German Balts and Russian journalists. These culminated in two pamphlets, one of which was an attack by the national-democrat and Slavophile aristocrat, J. F. Samarin and the other the 'Livonian Answer' from the Dorpat professor, C. Schirren (1869).

The position of the Baltic provinces was complicated by the legal regulations regarding religious denominations in Russia, according to which conversion to the Greek Orthodox Church could not be renounced. The children of mixed marriages had to attend the State Church and Protestant ministers were liable to prosecution for offering their ministry to the so-called reconverted. After the practical toleration introduced in 1865 by Alexander II, the strict mixed marriage regulations were again enforced by Alexander III in 1885, bringing five-sixths of the Protestant clergy of Livonia into conflict with the law. Only with the accession of Nicholas II were most of the 199 'pastor cases' dropped.

At the same time as national minorities were being Germanized and Magyarized in Germany and Hungary respectively Russia sought to assimilate her national minorities in the Baltic provinces between 1885 and 1893. The language of public authorities, the administration of justice, the university and all schools were Russified. In the long term this was bound to lead to the alienation of the affected population, even of the Estonians and Letts, whose national spokesmen hoped at the beginning – not without reason – that they would find in the Russian authorities an ally against the German ruling class.

Finland's fate demonstrated that the attempt to make a unified national state out of a multi-national empire led only to intensified national tensions: there at the beginning the Russian authorities had shown a willingness to compromise – in contrast to the repressive policies in rebellious Poland – and had allowed the Diet, which had been in abeyance since 1809, to meet in 1863. In the eighteenth century, 'henceforth ranking among the nations', as Alexander I had explained, Finland felt herself to be an affiliated state. She had her own ruling council, later a senate, her own recruitment arrangements, postal administration, from 1865 her own coinage and her own secretariat of state in St Petersburg to represent her interests there. Then came the interference from the Russian government, bringing a complete shake-up of the legal basis of the duchy: immediately after the appointment of General Bobrikov as governor-general in 1899 the 'Fundamental Laws' were issued. These aimed at the abolition of Finland's legal autonomy. The result was an address of protest containing more than half a million signatures in Finland and tremendous sympathy from the European intellectual world. Among the signatories to an address taken to St Petersburg in the summer of 1899 were

66 Russian peasants seizing Polish insurgents in the Dunaburg district, 1863. Engraving from Vilna, 1864.

Herbert Spencer, Anatole France, Emile Zola, Theodor Mommsen, Rudolf Virchow, Henrik Ibsen and Sven Hedin. But in spite of this the Russification policy was pursued and indeed – after a short-lived modification – was intensified during the revolutionary unrest during the Stolypin era. Finland, however, managed to preserve her independent political life in her own institutions – unlike Poland.

Of all the countries of non-Russian population and of old European culture incorporated by conquest in Russia, the kingdom or tsardom of Poland had the most tragic fate, both politically and nationally. After the repression of the 1863 rebellion Poland was cruelly punished. In addition her special position was abolished and she was assimilated culturally and administratively in Russia as the Vistula province. From 1865 Polish disappeared from the administration. How little pan-Slav community of interest really meant was shown at the Second pan-Slav congress in Moscow in 1867 in which not one Pole took part. Step by step the whole school system was Russified, a Russian university was founded in Warsaw (in 1869, twenty years before the Russification of Dorpat) and the judicature was assimilated to Russia's.

Agrarian reforms in Poland were carried out from a Russian nationalistic point of view and were intended to weaken the patriotic Polish aristocracy, although they did have the positive effect of strengthening the peasantry economically. The rise of industrial centres in Poland, Lodz among others, had far-reaching effects. Thanks to this there was a growth in the middle class and an ever greater growth in the industrial proletariat. Polish industry found 70–80 per cent of its markets in the Russian Empire, thus creating a Russo-Polish relationship on a different level. An expression of the new social situation and at the same time a sign of the strength of Polish nationalism was the development of Polish national democracy and the effectiveness of Roman Dmovski who proposed that Russia should be Poland's ally in the coming war with Germany.

It is not a matter for surprise that there was no room in the Russian National State, which received its stamp from the Great Russians, for the national endeavours of the Ukrainians. Where could all this lead? Anyone looking back today knows that in European nationalism, which its defenders among all peoples regarded as an essential factor for integration, that dynamic was working which led not only to the disruption of the old multi-national empires, but to the unreal expansion of sovereignty, to the expulsion of minorities and to the dissolution of spiritual bonds.

The time had passed when it could be said of the educated Russian that he spoke his own language only 'when he swears, prays or counts'. Pushkin (born 1799) showed Russian readers, thinkers and writers that in its expressive power and sonority Russian belonged to the literary languages of the world. Gogol, who died in 1852, a Ukrainian, through his own schizophrenic personality, opened up the whole of reality and more than reality. He finished the first volume of *Dead Souls* in Rome. 'Pushkin has created Russian literature, Gogol has put it on a definite path' (M. Braun). The following one and a half generations placed Russian literature among the classical possessions of European writing: Ivan Turgenev (born 1818), Fyodor Dostoyevsky (born 1821), Nikolai Nekrassov (born 1821), Count Leo Tolstoy (born 1828), Nikolai Leskov (born 1831). Over a generation younger were writers of equal stature; Anton Chekhov (born 1860), Maxim Gorky (born 1868), Ivan Bunin (born 1870, the first Russian Nobel Prize-winner for literature). No less a part of European literature are the younger writers: Alexander Blok (born 1880), Boris Pasternak (born 1890, Nobel Prize-winner), Mikhail Bulgakov (born 1891), Konstantin Paustovsky (born 1892), Vladimir Mayakovsky (born 1893), Mikhail Sholokhov (born 1905, Nobel Prize-winner), Alexander Solzhenitsyn (born 1918, Nobel Prize-winner). There are many more.

67, 68 A group of Russia's great men of letters. Left, Fyodor Dostoyevsky, 1880, right, Maxim Gorky, by I. Brodski, 1937. Tretyakov Gallery, Moscow.

It is absolutely impossible to show in a sketch of this kind what Europe meant for Russian literature and what it in turn meant for Europe. It is no exaggeration to say that not to know Russian literature is to know little of Russia. The converse is also true; familiarity with Russian writing from Pushkin to Gorky, from Blok to Solzhenitsyn is to have learnt much about Russia. Vladimir Weidlé once wrote: 'What is that – Russia? If anybody asked me this question after having woken me in the middle of the night, I should probably answer: Pushkin.'

In what lies the exceptional significance of literary representation? Can one really say that the newer writing from Russia shows more of Russia's relationship to Europe than an icon, a building, a historical picture, a folk-song or a symphony? The following considerations may help.

Solzhenitsyn's avowal in 1967 that 'a literature which cannot interpret the pain and the restlessness of society . . . does not deserve the name of literature' hangs like an inscription across two centuries of Russian writing. It is strange that a literary testimony with the standards of the European classics began in a country in which a thinly

69–72 Above left, Leo Tolstoy by I. Kramskoi, Tretiakov Gallery, Moscow. Above, Ivan Turgenev. Engraving by I. Pozhalostin. Museum of Literature, Moscow. Left, Anton Chekhov at Yalta, *c.* 1900. Below, Alexander Pushkin by O. Kiprensky.

spread educated class covered a mass of illiterate serfs. In Russia there were more disruptive tendencies than the State, which only as a centrally organized body could hold together that vast land, and the people, for whom the tsar was a myth, bureaucracy a burden. There was also the emancipated mind, only localized with difficulty, opposed to the State, drawn to the people in devoted love. 'The ruling class and the intellectuals were two very different things, but the people distrusted not just the State but also the evolving educated class and the repentant nobility' (V. Weidlé). That sharp-eyed critic of all things Russian, Victor Hehn, was told by a person with knowledge of the people that 'an educated Russian is an unhappy creature.' Was it a kind of double schizophrenia? the creative, even gifted madness of the writer?

At the same time sensuous vitality holds sway, unbroken, abolishing all social barriers. Reflections are translatable, love is not. Here the most mysterious elements of the Russian language are hidden, mocking all attempts at translation: the inexhaustible richness of the vowel sounds, the tenderness of diminutives, the hair-raising profanity and the unhypocritical humility. To translate words like *batyushka* or *dushen'ka*, *krugom vinovat* or *mrakobesie* is impossible and no foreign art can cross the innermost frontiers.

To understand the social criticism of the best Russian literature is to explain the accord between the public and the writer. It has been observed, rightly, that about the middle of the nineteenth century, especially during the time of the great reforms, the famous periodicals (like Nekrassov's *Sovremennik*) constituted 'a form of book production', that literature depended not on the power machine but on public opinion and that, conversely, literature made public opinion dependent on writing. Turgenev's *Fathers and Sons*, first published in the periodical *Russky Vyestnik* in 1862, is concerned with more than the generation gap. Its theme is as European as it is Russian, but it is not a precise characterization of the writer, who lived for many years in Western Europe, to say that he is too European. The medical student Bazarov, in Turgenev's most famous novel, stands unmistakably in a Russian environment and the girl Liza in *Gentry Nest*, one of the many charming young female creations of the writer and of Russian literature as such, can be what she is, like Lavretsky, only because she comes from the Russian gentry. Of course the aristocratic way of life, in so far as it had common European characteristics, was easier for the foreigner to understand than Leskov's *The Cathedral Folk* (1872) or the Cossack world of Sholokhov's *And Quiet flows the Don*.

In their artistic and intellectual power Tolstoy and Dostoyevsky transcend the framework of the theme 'Russia and Europe'. Suffice it to say here that each of them, influenced by his background, walked along the literary heights and transmuted Russia's Christian traditions. But as philosophically minded writers they could not but show traces of their era and its intellectual secularization. Yet the broad understanding of the one and the deep penetration of the other opened up those realms of the soul wherein both Russia and Europe could recognize themselves, in their own time, today and in the future (M. Doerne).

By this, of course, is not meant that romantic trait which made many disappointed Central and West Europeans seek for the land of the undefiled soul in archaic Russia. Among those pilgrims was the young German poet from Bohemia, Rainer Maria Rilke, who paid a visit to Tolstoy on his estate about the turn of the century and who was overpowered by Russia, her vastness, her simplicity and originality. The great polite old gentlemanly earth-spirit at Yasnaya Polyana must have smiled somewhat embarrassed at the stammering hyperbole of this twenty-four-year-old.

When Bismarck was Prussian envoy at St Petersburg he was astonished by the nationalistic and revolutionary mood of society there: 'The educated classes and the officers', he wrote in October 1860, a few months before the emancipation of the serfs, 'are noisiest in criticism'. Everyone admired Garibaldi. In January 1861 Bismarck reported that the whole of the peasant population was dissatisfied and had exaggerated expectations of the impending reforms; the aristocracy was embittered and there were 'no fewer people here than in other countries . . . who work systematically for the overthrow of the political establishment'. After emancipation this alert observer noted the disorders throughout the country, the executions and the fusillades. Gifted radical writers were writing in periodicals and in pamphlets, though for the time being without deeper effect. The first attempt to assassinate the emperor was made in April 1866. The culprit was a student. A peasant was supposed to have saved the emperor's life and was rewarded by being ennobled. The extraordinary fate of this 'tsar saver' was described with biting irony in Victor Hehn's posthumously published diary (*De moribus Ruthenorum*). 'The veneration of the tsar is still deeply rooted here', but 'the Asiatic must be kept on a tight rein or he capers about'. The Asiatic? The first spokesmen of the Russian revolutionary movement were European-educated Russians. It is a thought worth savouring that the most effective of European anarchists were two Russian aristocrats, educated in the old European style; Mikhail Bakunin, the 'aesthete of destruction', the philosopher of the 'traditionless slavonic muddle' (P. Scheibert), and Prince Peter Kropotkin, page in the imperial household, officer, scholarly geographer, famous refugee, agitator in Geneva and in France. He who has come to know the present-day omnipotent State will appreciate a little better Kropotkin's passionate denunciations. Coming from a Russia rooted in absolutism and centralism he saw rise on a world scale something horrifying which was the very negation of freedom. 'The state crushes the personality and regional life, takes control of all areas of human activity, introduces war and the struggle for power into internal affairs, brings superficial revolutions which mean no more than a change of tyrants and death as an inevitable end' (1896). The kernel of Kropotkin's positive alternative was 'the highest development of voluntary association', a principle which can be recognized in the pre-absolutist phase of European history as much as in Russia's co-operative institutions. Kropotkin's ideal, it might be said, was mainly of Russian origin.

The weakness of the anarchists' schemes were wittily mocked by the Russian Marxist G. Plekhanov. Bakunin was expelled from the International. In Russia the revolutionary movement, springing from the intelligentsia and supported by it, sought different forms of action. After the romantic and idealistic beginning of the 'going to the people' movement, the attempt of thousands of enthusiasts, young and old, to spread enlightenment among the broad masses and to awaken revolutionary consciousness, the secret revolutionary organization *Zemlya i volya*, 'Land and Freedom', was formed in 1876. The aims of this movement, the *narodnichestvo*, populism, became known throughout Europe after 1877 through numerous criminal proceedings by the misleading literary name 'nihilism'. D. M. Wallace in his famous book on Russia (first published in 1877) wrote: 'Roughly speaking, the Nihilist movement in Russia may be described as the exaggerated, distorted reflection of the earlier Socialist movements of the West; but it has local peculiarities and local colouring which deserve attention.' That was also A. Leroy-Beaulieu's opinion in *L'Empire des Tsars et les Russes* (1881–82): nihilism was – despite its extraordinary symptoms – only the Russian form of the negative and revolutionary spirit of the century. The German envoy General von Schweinitz noted in 1877 that the programme was presented in a European form and was original but that its prophets were 'unselfish, fearless, true to their convictions . . . ignorant but gifted, often incapable of writing but able to speak in a way which surpasses the eloquence of the advocate'. In all these Western European impressions the same embarrassment can be detected, Europe recognizes herself in the ideas but much is different.

At the end of January 1878 the military governor of St Petersburg was shot and wounded by Vera Zasulich, the daughter of a general. This was followed, after her sensational acquittal and another attempt to arrest her and her successful flight, by one terror attack after another. In autumn 1879 on the foundation of the *Narodnaya volya* (Will of the People) group a systematic all-out attempt on the emperor's life began, ending, as is well known, in his murder in March 1881.

The death of Alexander II closed the path which would have led Russia, if not yet to parliamentary institutions then to a central, indirect advisory representative body which had already been approved by the emperor. The harsh autocracy of Alexander III supported by the State Church's chief procurator, Pobedonostsev, showed that a series of murders did not start a revolution. But the struggle between the governmental system and the revolutionary movement acquired the character of a life-and-death struggle, with morally depraving effects. The government's unscrupulous informer network and police system was paralleled by the slow decline of all moral inhibitions in the opposition groups. In her memoirs Vera Zasulich related how the much admired terrorist, S. M. Kravchinsky (Stepnyak), professed, like Danton, that the rape of one's own moral sense could be a heroic deed.

The reception of Karl Marx's teaching was the most momentous event in Russia's later history. It was a complex process, full of tensions and by no means straightforward, which cannot be discussed here. Russia had the most important requisites, the existence of non-bourgeois, socio-critical, anti-state groups of intelligentsia, passionately inclined towards theory and fully understanding the importance of the rise of capitalism and industry as well as the rise of the industrial proletariat. The great illegal strikes in St Petersburg in 1896 and 1897 were symptoms of a radical and imminent change in the entire social and economic structure. Many members of the intelligentsia in the 1890s only went through a Marxist phase and were not influenced by it for long, people such as Berdyaev, Bulgakov, P. Struve, the writer I. Bunin and the economic historian Tugan-Baranovsky. Marx himself took great interest in Russian conditions and devoted much study to them. After careful deliberation his cautious answer to Vera Zasulich's disquieting question on the social function of the village commune was conditional though not unsympathetic.

Because of political events it was unavoidable that the theoretical formation of Russian Marxism took place among the emigrés (G. V. Plekhanov, P. B. Axelrod, Vera Zasulich, J. O. Martov) or at first in a place of banishment in Siberia and then abroad (Vladimir Ilyich Ulyanov: Lenin). Those who took part in the First Party Congress of the Russian Social-Democratic Workers' Party in Minsk in 1898 were almost all immediately arrested. The Second Congress (1903) opened in Brussels but was soon transferred to London. This was the hour of birth of Bolshevism and Menshevism and at first the congress was overshadowed by the depressing ideological squabbles of emigrés living in overcrowded conditions, as Lenin later wrote, squabbles which changed immediately into personal animosities. The conciliatory attempts of the German Social Democrats which originated of course from the Mensheviks was spurned by Lenin, though much later his idea of a centrally controlled tightly knit party did show itself to be the more effective one. If up to World War I social democracy in Russia did not succeed – except during the revolutionary year 1905 – in overcoming a certain narrowmindedness the reasons were (as has been shown by research) the continued existence of Russian absolutism (D. Geyer). The State, always stronger than society in Russia, kept in its hands the means of keeping out of the public eye the strongest intellectual forces of the Revolution.

Those Russian émigrés whose fate was even more bitter than exile in Siberia had without doubt read widely and learned much in English, French and German. They had studied socialism from a wider horizon than their intellectual comrades in the individual countries in which they led their lonely lives. But all their endeavours and aspirations, their thoughts and hopes were turned towards Russia. This was

Lenin addressing Red Army soldiers leaving for the Polish front, 5 May 1920. Painting by I. Brodski.

also true for Lenin, the greatest, most consistent and most universal of them. This man stemmed from the Russian intelligentsia and was through his father a member of the ennobled official class but already in early youth he had broken through his environmental boundaries.

He has been called an 'absolutely un-Russian type of Russian intellectual' and it is certain that his exceptional willpower was rare among Russian theorists. His enemy Chernov, a social revolutionary and president of the Russian Constitutional Assembly, which was broken up in 1918 by Lenin, said of him in 1917: 'Lenin has an imposing wholeness. He is as complete as if made from a piece of granite, as roundly lathed as a billiard ball. There is no getting a grip on him, he rolls forward relentlessly. He has an unusual intelligence but it is a "one-dimensional" one, even one-tracked.' But Chernov's milieu-theory is an illusion, for the new Russian life would cut down to size this 'interesting political figure'. It is ridiculous to suppose that it could be the other way round. But was Lenin un-Russian? It is irrelevant to bring into consideration his German ancestry (on his mother's side) or his Kalmuk blood (from his grandmother). Russia has produced systematizers as well as strong-willed natures. The game of chess was 'almost a Russian game' and the hundreds of peasant revolts were inconceivable without extreme determination. To see how Lenin in his writing mingled European concepts and a Russian outlook, how he wrote and spoke and how spontaneously he referred to the way of life, historical and contemporary of the Russian world is to be in no doubt about his 'Russianness'.

Again and again the publications of émigrés in Western Europe have had a revolutionary influence on Russia. That was true of Herzen's *Kolokol*, as well as of the Social Democratic *Iskra* (The Spark) which from 1900 on was printed successively in Leipzig, Munich, London and Geneva. The same means were also used by the radical activists of the *Zemstvo* movement. During a congress of cottage industry workers in St Petersburg in March 1902 it was decided to publish abroad a periodical critical both of the State and society and that summer P. Struve began to publish the fortnightly *Osvobozhdenie* (Liberation) in Stuttgart, later moving to Paris. At first its programme was a negative, 'away with the autocracy' one and it professed, for tactical reasons, sympathies with the revolutionary movement, its aims and its policy of force. The *Revolyutsionnaya Rossiya* (Revolutionary Russia) which appeared from 1902 onwards was the central voice of the party of the Social Revolutionaries which had been founded in 1901 in the tradition of the *narodnichestvo*. Dissatisfaction in Russia spread wider and wider after the Russo-Japanese War. During it all those opposed to the regime wished for Russia's defeat. Terrorism came into its own again: In August 1904 the minister of the interior Pleve, was murdered, as his predecessor Sipyagin was in 1902.

One of the most important indications of the internal political situation in Russia at the beginning of the century was the radicalization of the student bodies, an event which was in tune with all the other factors of the historical process and which had few parallels in the rest of Europe at that time. The government used troops and police against the students' mass demonstrations in St Petersburg in 1901 and in Moscow in 1902. Social and economic elements as well as the current state of Russia's scientific knowledge would have to be considered in seeking an explanation for these events.

What Russian science achieved in the nineteenth and twentieth centuries and how it compared with that of Western Europe has not been given much attention in this outline. It seems that it retained from the period of the Enlightenment a strong pragmatic and positive approach. One as individualistic and as outstanding as the philosopher Vladimir Soloviev (died 1900) does not negate this hypothesis. Soloviev himself had pointed out dryly in 1888 that the Russians had until then 'understood foreign philosophical ideas very well', had assimilated them but had not produced any important philosophical work of their own. Recently it has become recognized that Soloviev's creative work 'anticipated almost all the methodological instruments of German phenomenology, at least in their beginnings' (H. Dahm). Vladimir Soloviev belongs – as well as the above mentioned poets, Chekhov, Gorky, Bunin, Blok and many others – to the 'Silver Age' of Russian culture which brought a renaissance in almost all fields of spiritual and artistic life during the twenty years preceding World War I.

It is not easy to track Russia's path towards the revolution of 1905. As in essence it was an internal Russian process a few comments must suffice.

In 1904 the *Zemstvo* movement became one of the strongest influences working for a change in the system and it saw practical prospects after Pleve's death in August 1904 when the new minister of the interior, Prince P. D. Svyatopolk-Mirsky, declared his intention of working in harness with the social institutions. It was a serious reverse when in December the emperor's other advisers refused to support his bill. The ministry of the interior was no longer able to control the workers' organizations which had been set up by the police department so as to defuse agitation in the factories by supporting some of the workers' demands. Now these organizations themselves were becoming more and more influenced by revolutionary demands. What happened to these so-called *Zubatovshchina* was a new phenomenon in Russia as was the radicalization of the *Zemstvo* movement. The ancient over-powerful State appeared to have been lifted off its hinges by the dynamic of social change. The sick joke about 'Russian despotism being softened by foul murder' did not appear to point to the future.

The revolution began with the incidents of Bloody Sunday, 22 January 1905, in St Petersburg when a peaceable mass parade was turned into a blood bath. It was privately estimated that about a thousand men, women and children were killed when the crowd was fired on by troops. Carelessness, fear, the crumbling of the State apparatus and that stupid and unreflective use of force for which an autocratic power trains its servants were responsible for the outrage. It is not surprising that Lenin immediately suspected government provocation, that the regime had goaded the proletariat into a revolt so as to smother it in a sea of blood.

It is a matter of dispute if the concessions extorted from the regime after the 1905 revolution amounted to a 'pseudo-constitutionalism' (Max Weber). The term is not altogether apposite; if it were then a pseudo-parliamentary representation would have to be ascribed to those countries (e.g. Germany) which lacked ministerial responsibility. Yet there are some good reasons why the term might be applicable to Russian conditions: the emperor's prerogatives were still unusually great. More important, the government had already broken the constitution brought in by themselves and had missed it on a second occasion. On 16 June 1907 it deliberately violated the constitution by changing the electoral law, knowing that it could not expect collaboration from the Duma without changing both its social and political balance. Then again, in 1911, Stolypin's manipulation of the Duma in pushing through the *Zemstvo* law for the West province (former Polish territory) had most of the characteristics of a *coup d'état*.

74 'The Eleventh Hour', *Punch* cartoon by Linley Sambourne, 15 November 1905, referring to 'Bloody Sunday' 22 January 1905, and the granting of a constitution by Nicholas II.

THE ELEVENTH HOUR.

Shade of King Louis the Sixteenth (*to the* Czar). "SIDE WITH YOUR PEOPLE, SIRE, WHILE THERE IS YET TIME. *I* WAS TOO LATE!"

But this act and many others showed that the Duma consisted not only of government henchmen. As a protest against the apparently legal though forceful operation of the *Zemstvo* law Guchkov, the president of the Duma, resigned. When in 1908 the minister of finance, Kokovtsov, allowed himself to be carried away with the remark that 'Thank God, we have no parliament yet' it evoked loud indignation from the parliamentary representatives. There was a strong minority of the parties, from the Constitutional Democrats (KD, Kadety) to the Social Democrats, in opposition. Several attempts to engage the KD Party in government failed because the opposition demanded full parliamentary powers.

To be fair it must be admitted that many an opponent of a transfer of Western European constitutional models to Russia cannot be

151

labelled as un-European obscurantists. There were in the Duma, the intelligentsia and the bureaucracy many Anglophiles, for whom English political life had a strong attraction. Many honest advocates of Russia's assimilation to modern political forms believed – not without reason – that it must be preceded by the raising of the educational standards of the masses; for the vast mass of the population was still illiterate.

Above all, two points can be made against the attitudes associated with the term 'sham constitutionalism': from the founding of the Duma in 1906, not only in the first two but also, after the changes in the electoral law, in the third and fourth Dumas there was a forum for open criticism and with that a factor for the development of political awareness which should not be underestimated. In the preparation of legislation the Duma became so experienced over the years as to become a first-class training ground for detailed parliamentary work. Russia's transition from an autocracy to a constitutional monarchy became an undoubted fact, despite many upsets.

But the October Manifesto of 30 October 1905, which marked that transition and gave the people so-called civil liberties, was accepted only with the greatest reluctance by Nicholas II. On the other hand its reception by the people was astonishingly favourable, except from the extreme conservatives and the revolutionary groups. But then the Social Revolutionaries and the Social Democrats had begun preparations for an armed revolt long before this. It broke out in Moscow in December 1905 and was quickly suppressed, though it took over a year for the authorities to round up suspects and stamp out the anarchy which had reigned in certain regions. Trial by court martial and heavy punishments restored order.

Firstly in the provinces and then in St Petersburg an institution evolved which though developed from strike committees was based on the old Russian tradition of self-help still flourishing among manual workers. This was the Soviet of Workers' Deputies, a pointer to the future. In the main cities it became a political body of representatives and in its executive committees the centre of the revolutionary movement. In St Petersburg the Soviet came under Menshevik influence, in Moscow the Bolsheviks controlled it.

During the following years the State apparatus grew stronger again, supported by the police who used all possible means, illegal and demoralizing ones, too, even anti-Semitic outbursts. The police informer network reached far into the revolutionary organizations. Several cases became known to the public, the most important the corruption of the Bolshevik leader in the fourth Duma, Malinovsky, who was at the same time an agent of the security police.

Despite this, attempted assassinations continued. Workers' strikes which had dropped heavily in 1906–10 began to increase again in 1912, reaching a million strikers in the first six months of 1914, equalling the total for the revolutionary year 1905.

If the question is asked whether or not Russia was ripe for revolution in 1914 the answer can hardly be positive. Trotsky, looking back, was sceptical. Lenin in May 1917 wrote that 'if the war had not come Russia could have lived for years, even decades, without a revolution against the capitalists'. The peasantry, in a state of rapid change, could not have become a threat to a strong regime. Industrial development based on a capitalist economy had wide possibilities, and since the revolution of 1905 society had become activated and was in a state of evolution. It was not nonsensical to think, as some did, that the old empire might take the 'American' road.

Not all were equally affected by the war. Of those peasants liable for military service only 60 per cent were called up. The decrease in tillage did not reach a dangerous level. Nor was there any question of hunger despite great social and geographical differences in the empire. As almost all grain exports ceased the necessary amount of bread could have been produced. The hunger in the large cities from the autumn of 1916 onwards was largely the result of the collapse of the transport system, brought to straining-point by the war and the confused direction of the responsible authorities. As in other countries, the disproportionately high profits made in industry during the war provoked the sharpest reaction. And the living standard of the workers remained too low compared with their long hours of work. The loss of authority by the imperial couple was compounded by some mistakes of their own, including the toleration of Rasputin, and by the mistrust of them which was systematically aroused by the opposition. Yet the progressive bloc in the Duma, formed in 1915, did not desire the fall of the emperor, though they did demand a 'ministry of social trust'.

Despite the conventional explanations the revolution of March 1917 was not a middle-class revolution. It was a revolt caused by the elementary wants of the Petrograd masses and it quickly succeeded

153

75 Prince Lvov, who headed the provisional government in Russia in 1917 from March to July.

because the bulk of the garrison troops joined the workers. Two-thirds of the Soviet of Workers' and Soldiers' Deputies, which was immediately set up, consisted of soldiers.

The Provisional Government, which according to socialist theory must be called a middle-class government, had not one single socialist in the cabinet apart from Alexander Kerensky, the minister of justice. But sociologically an exact description cannot be given using Western European terminology. Of the three capitalist members one, Guchkov, was without influence and soon resigned. A second, Tereshchenko, was in favour of co-operating with the socialists while the third, Konovalov, was so opposed to his own class that he resigned. The prime minister Prince Lvov declared himself in favour of the break-up of the large estates for the benefit of the peasants and he was among those who in May 1917 brought about the coalition government with the Mensheviks, Social Revolutionaries and the People's Socialists. Russia was the first European country in which 40 per cent of a government were socialists.

Freedom was both the Credo and the Pathos of the Provisional Government. When Lenin, returning from Switzerland via Germany, issued his *April Theses* he declared under point 2 that of all the countries engaged in the war Russia was most free. His theory of revolution demanded the most rigorous action against compromise with the capitalists and bourgeoisie; for his goal was the dictatorship of the proletariat. The Mensheviks, the most important of whom was I. G. Tsereteli, wanted to reach socialism by easy stages as against Lenin who wished to get there as quickly as possible. The main reason for the attitude of the Mensheviks was their belief that a separate peace with the Central Powers was unacceptable to Russia. Therefore, they argued, war material should have first preference. As far as they were concerned there was no need for the British and French delegations (among them A. Thomas and A. Henderson) which came to convince the Russian socialists of the necessity of continuing the war. The entrance of the USA into the war was decisive in that it blocked

76 Dnieper power station, 1937 poster, with 'Lenin the Technocrat' portrayed as inspiration. British Museum.

Russia's quest for neutrality, although the non-Bolshevik socialists sought to get general peace talks under way.

Taking over as prime minister from Prince Lvov in July 1917 Kerensky, as is well known, succeeded in isolating himself through his maladroit and opportunistic approach. Among the masses the Mensheviks lost much ground to the Bolsheviks, while the Social Revolutionaries maintained their position among the peasants. In the elections for the Constituent Assembly, held after the revolution, most of the 69·6 per cent anti-Bolshevik vote came from the Social Revolutionaries.

In the Dissolution Decree Lenin defended his disruption of the Constituent Assembly in 1918 by arguing that the people had not been able to choose between the right-wing Social Revolutionaries, the followers of the bourgeoisie, and the left-wing social revolutionaries, the followers of socialism. What can one make of this? Was it possible at this time that in the vast breadth of Russia democratic elections could not represent a fully rational expression of the will of the Russian people? Was the euphoria of freedom but a dream? Was Russia too European and at the same time not European enough? Such questions peg the boundaries of our theme.

EPILOGUE

Today the visitor from Leningrad to Petrodvorets stands before Peter the Great's palace, Peterhof, dazzled by this lovely monument of European-Russian architecture with its numerous shimmering fountains and gilded statues, its well-tended Baroque park and the canal connecting it with the Gulf of Finland. Yet the palace is new, rebuilt by the Soviet authorities after its destruction in Hitler's invasion. The reconstruction of such a representative exemplar of the imperial past tempts one to forget the differences which separate the Soviet State from Imperial Russia.

But it is just the lack of embarrassment shown by the Leninist State in its restoration of such reminders of the dynasty which demonstrates how deeply Old Russia is buried in the past. Now it is nothing more than a memory. The deep divide created by the October revolution and the four long years of civil war has created a break with the past which in the fifty years of Soviet rule has become absolute.

Swept away utterly was the aristocratic ruling class with its European upbringing and its Russian lifestyle, as was the small wealthy entrepreneur class; the large many-runged imperial bureaucracy; the intelligentsia, intellectually emancipated, revolutionary or semi-revolutionary in spirit; what remained of the patriarchal peasantry; the golden glow of the State Church. The whole social fabric of Imperial Russia was swept away. Or was it? Does not the tradition of struggle in the enlarged working class provide continuity with the past? Has not the spirit of freedom which distinguished the Russian intelligentsia emerged again in the artistic revolt against the regimented literary policy of the Communist Party? Its manifestations from Boris Pasternak, who was forced to refuse the Nobel Prize in 1958, to Alexander Solzhenitsyn, who had to renounce the presentation of the Nobel Prize in Stockholm in 1970, have aroused the sympathy of half the world. Are there not Old Russian influences still at work within the peasantry – in spite of the mechanization of agriculture and the change-over to *kolkhoz* and *sovkhoz*?

77 The first tractor, etching by V. Petrov to illustrate salvation through technology, from the catalogue of the Jubilee exhibition of Ukrainian art, 1970.

The upheaval experienced by the peasantry since 1930 has been described in official Soviet historiography as an 'extremely deep revolutionary change' which was 'comparable in its consequences' with the October revolution. The collectivization of the individual holdings of the peasantry was linked with the 'liquidation' of the independent and economically strong kulak class, as laid down in Stalin's programme in December 1929. Although by 1939 almost all agriculture had been organized into collectives the deportation, pauperization and somatic destruction of the better-off and middle-income peasants was answered by obstruction to tillage programmes and by the killing of livestock. The result was famine. Parallel with this development went State-enforced and accelerated industrialization with an enormous increase in the production of steel, coal, crude oil and electricity and a one-sided promotion of heavy industry, especially armaments. But all this was at the expense of consumer durables.

As a result the social landscape has undergone a fundamental change. Millions of peasants moved into rapidly expanding towns, millions more became employees of mechanized agricultural units. The so-called 'practical intelligentsia', divided into various categories and grades and made up of millions of experts of all kinds, proliferated, depending on a state and party apparatus which in turn needs its support. Industrial development and social change increased rapidly after heavy initial set-backs and the loss of an estimated seventeen million lives in the war against Hitler. In the modern industrial state which the Soviet Union is today more than one-third of the labour force still works on the land. But this is no longer the old peasantry.

Apart from the state of emergency during the war the dictatorship of the Communist Party was, in the Stalin era, legally anchored in the constitution (1936). The party forms the ruling nucleus of all workers' organizations, social as well as public, while basic rights recognized in the constitution cannot be exercised unless they coincide with 'the workers' interests' and contribute to 'the strengthening of socialist order'. The acceptance of the general ideological line is assured through the monopoly of political debate, education and the formation of public opinion and the use of trials, supervision, imprisonment and isolation, internment camps, compulsory transfer, withdrawal of permission to practice one's profession and exile.

After thirteen journeys in the Soviet Union (1929–59) Klaus Mehnert, one of the leading German experts on Russia, concluded that present-day 'Soviet man' accepts the authority of the State, the primacy of discipline and the superior wisdom of the closed ruling group. Mehnert traced the power of obedience, the docility, willing or unwilling, not only to the omnipotence of the police and the influence of a monopolized propaganda but to the psychological conditioning of a centuries-old tradition and its uninterrupted use. Does the dictatorship of the party stand on the shoulders of tsarist autocracy and the bureaucracy of imperial times?

Much could be said in support of this: especially when it is considered that even the improvement in educational standards and the disappearance of illiteracy have not, apparently, changed basic

78 'The Illiterate is like a blind man – misfortune and bad luck await him.' Poster by A. Radakov. Lords Gallery, London.

НЕГРАМОТНЫЙ тот-же СЛЕПОЙ
ВСЮДУ ЕГО ЖДУТ НЕУДАЧИ И НЕСЧАСТЬЯ·

attitudes. But in the field of education the progress brought about by the Soviet government is obvious and indisputable. The whole educational system has been raised to new levels, in all its branches and stages despite extreme difficulties and diverging aims. Of course disciplined teaching is accompanied by systematic indoctrination which makes lifelong devotion to Communist ideology the accepted thing for those passing through the educational system. At all age levels there is a remarkable eagerness to learn. In queues before kiosks and on benches in public parks adults can be seen reading, not illustrated magazines for those scarcely exist, but manuals, textbooks or classical novels. The natural sciences and engineering are representative of Russian science. Astronautics is of world class while armament technology is equal to the best. There is no doubt about the self-assurance of the scientific-technical intelligentsia.

What stabilizes the supremacy of the party and its ruling cadres is not just the Old Russian tradition of obedience but primarily the application of technology to the exercise of power. Imperial Russia applied press censorship and had a police force which used sophisticated methods, but at that time the film was in its infancy, radio and television were unknown and governmental economic management was far less effective than the Soviet five-year plans. The aeroplane, the motor car and telecommunications were not available to exercise control over this vast empire. In his Russian book *Zadacha Rossii* (Russia's Task, 1956) the Russian émigré, art historian and philosopher Vladimir Weidlé attributed – in a loving sketch of Old Russia – three achievements to the revolution: the consciousness of the unity of the whole immense country, the participation of the entire population in its historic life and a ruling class which is in touch with the people and not estranged from them internally. It was to the advantage of the Soviet regime that it overcame its difficulties just at the time when modern technology made its last qualitative leap and developed a charismatic quality along with visible progress, giving the State, which identifies with it, an added potential. To the application of technology to power is added the power of technology.

The significance of opposition within Russia is difficult to assess. Its power is not political. Guesses about the extent and internal attractiveness of Russian Christendom *vis-à-vis* official atheism are even more difficult to make. Christianity is alive but can it form opinion? Is there any point in reminding one of the words of the Muscovite

Metropolitan Philaret which Gogol noted: that in the Russian people there is 'little light but much warmth'. Since even the most remote village has been touched by the new enlightenment the accepted standards are not those which were valid during the period of illiteracy. Did Stalin's dictum touch the heart of the matter when he said that revolutionary Russia applies wide-ranging Russian inspiration (*russky razmakh*) to American routine (*amerikanskaya delovitost*)?

The relationship of contemporary Russia to the rest of Europe is ambivalent. Nothing is heard now of the spiritual *Angst* of the Slavophiles or Old Believers. Never before were so many millions of Russians learning English and German. Geoffrey Barraclough says – in contrast to the views of A. J. Toynbee – that 'the values of Soviet communism, as expressed in Marxist doctrine, are Western values. . . .' Wherever in European or Asiatic Russia power stations, industrial complexes, modern universities and new residential quarters are developed, the landscape is altered in much the same way as in other parts of the world where technology is at work. Assimilation is unmistakable. But is it assimilation with Europe? Is it not just a change similar to that which grips one European country after another, one continent after another? The European origin of worldwide technical change is nothing more than a historical fact.

Official information about the Western world as doled out to the Soviet people is scanty, fragmentary and ideologically coloured. Extremely few Russians are in a position to form their own opinions by visits to the capitalist West, while Western tourist groups visiting Russia make few and ephemeral contacts.

Is not the traditional confrontation between 'Russia and Europe' invalid and obsolete? Russia has assimilated everything 'Western' but cannot become more 'European' because the Europe which confronted her for centuries no longer exists. American world power is not part of Europe even though it stands on European soil.

The old Russia was not only a 'European' power, and in the form of that mighty and resilient *panzer*, the Soviet Union, she now is a world power and, since her triumphant victory over Hitler's Germany, has controlled or ruled over more of the rest of Europe than Imperial Russia ever did. The Soviet Union has incorporated the Baltic states, which gained their independence in 1918–19; the former eastern provinces of Poland, and Moldavia. Königsberg in East Prussia is under Soviet rule. Along with the former Allied powers the Soviet

Union has rights of control over Berlin. When called upon Moscow's *panzer* divisions can regulate political events in Czechoslovakia. Her East European allies strengthen the Eastern Bloc to which such old European cities as Warsaw, Cracow, Breslau, Leipzig and Prague belong. It is difficult to estimate how much the shock of the German invasion of 1941 – the fourth invasion from the West after Poland's in 1610, Charles XII in 1708/9 and Napoleon's in 1812 – influences present-day security policy in the Soviet Union.

Who would dare forecast the future relationship of the Soviet Union with China, the rising third world power? It may be argued that in spite of their power rivalry these two giants are united by their common ideology. But the European looking towards the Far East perceives – despite the ideological connection between these two powers – the European character of Moscow's historical position. The frontier of Europe is the Amur.

In discussing the relationship between Russia and Europe care must be taken not to claim for Europe forces which – like science and technology – have become the property of all mankind or which – like Christianity – have neither originated in Europe nor were confined to it. Konstantin Nikolaevich Leontiev (who died in 1891), the Russian conservative thinker, who shortly before his death secretly became a monk at the famous Optina Pustyn, had a bitter foreboding which offended his aristocratic taste: today's revolution is a period neither of terror nor lawlessness. 'The revolution of our time is the striving towards a general uniform type, towards an average harmless industrious but unbelieving man who is part epicurean, part stoic.'

The worldwide process of levelling down must not cause us to shut our eyes to the lasting differences which exist not only between 'East' and 'West', but between Eastern Europe's political and social system and the pluralist society of Western Europe. Nor can we shut our eyes to the disruptive tensions within old Europe.

79 Kalinin Avenue. 'A taste of honey for >
Muscovites'. The old and the new.

MAPS

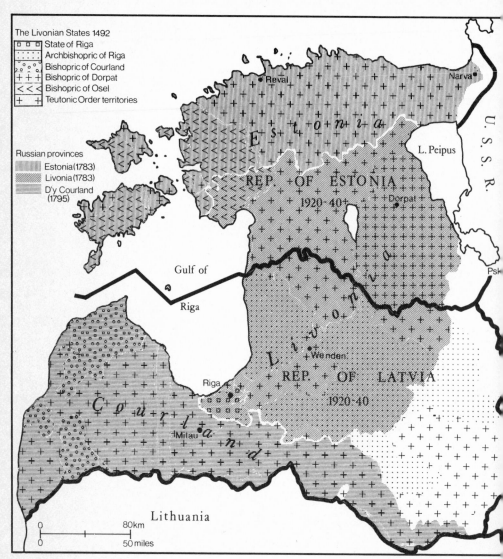

The Livonian States 1492
- ▢ ▢ ▢ State of Riga
- ∵ ∵ ∵ Archbishopric of Riga
- °₀°₀° Bishopric of Courland
- + + + Bishopric of Dorpat
- < < < Bishopric of Osel
- + + Teutonic Order territories

Russian provinces
- Estonia (1783)
- Livonia (1783)
- D'y Courland (1795)

Reval • Narva

E s t o n i a

L. Peipus

U. S. S. R.

REP. + OF ESTONIA
1920-40 • Dorpat

Psl

Gulf of

Riga

L i v o n i a

• Wenden

REP. + OF LATVIA
1920-40

C o u r l a n d
Riga •
Mitau •

Lithuania

0   80km
0   50 miles

80 Baltic lands.

400 km

250 miles

Borders of 1920

81 European invasions of Russia.

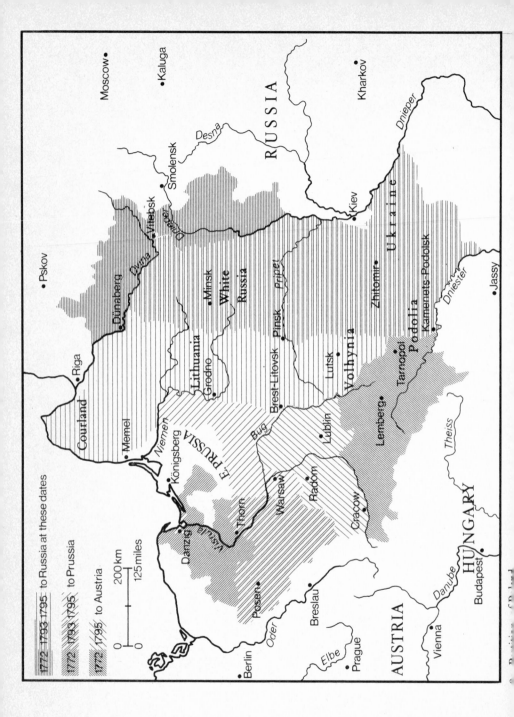

1772 1793 1795 to Russia at these dates

1772 1793 1795 to Prussia

1772 1795 to Austria

200 km
125 miles

Moscow
Kaluga
RUSSIA
Kharkov
Desna
Smolensk
Vitebsk
Dnieper
Pskov
Dvina
Dünaberg
Kiev
Ukraine
Riga
Courland
Minsk
White
Russia
Pripet
Zhitomir
Dniester
Jassy
Memel
Lithuania
Grodno
Pinsk
Brest-Litovsk
Volhynia
Lutsk
Tarnopol
Podolia
Kamenets-Podolsk
Königsberg
E. PRUSSIA
Niemen
Bug
Lublin
Lemberg
Thorn
Warsaw
Radom
Cracow
Danzig
Vistula
Posen
Breslau
Oder
HUNGARY
Theiss
Berlin
Prague
Elbe
AUSTRIA
Vienna
Budapest
Danube

8   Partition of Poland

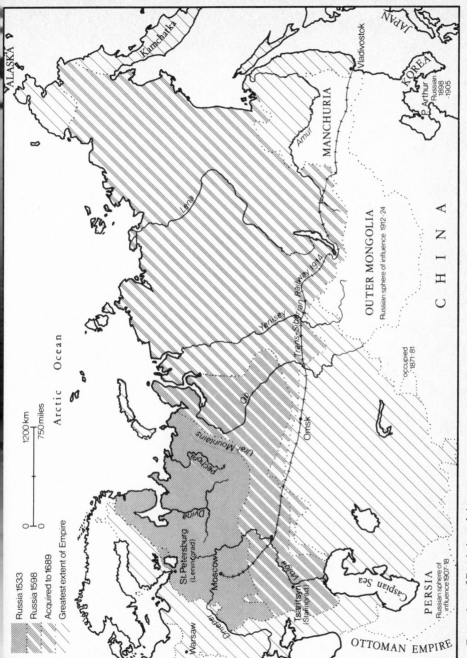

Russia 1533
Russia 1598
Acquired to 1689
Greatest extent of Empire

Arctic   Ocean

0   1200 km
0   750 miles

ALASKA

Kamchatka

Lena

Yenisey

Trans-Siberian Railway 1914

Ob

Ural Mountains

Omsk

Pechora

Dvina

St Petersburg
(Leningrad)

Moscow

Warsaw

Dnieper

Don

Volga

Tsaritsyn
(Stalingrad)

Caspian Sea

OTTOMAN EMPIRE

PERSIA

Russian sphere of
influence 1907-18

occupied
1871-81

CHINA

OUTER MONGOLIA

Russian sphere of influence 1912-24

MANCHURIA

Amur

Vladivostok

P. Arthur
Russian
1898
-1905

KOREA

JAPAN

83 Expansion of Russia into Asia.

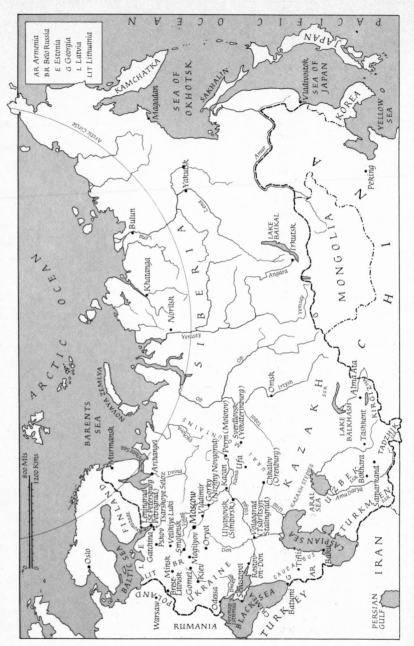

AR Armenia
BR Belo Russia
E Estonia
G Georgia
L Latvia
LIT Lithuania

PACIFIC OCEAN

ARCTIC OCEAN

Arctic Circle

KAMCHATKA

SEA OF
OKHOTSK

SAKHALIN

JAPAN

Magadan

Vladivostok

SEA OF
JAPAN

KOREA

YELLOW
SEA

Yakutsk

Amur

Bulun

Lena

Lena

Peking

MONGOLIA

Khatanga

S I B E R I A

LAKE
BAIKAL

Irkutsk

Noriilsk

Angara

C H I N A

Yenisey

Yenisey

BARENTS
SEA

NOVAYA ZEMLYA

Ob

Ob

Irtysh

Omsk

Tobol

Murmansk

White Sea

KAZAKH SSR

Alma Ata

LAKE
BALKHASH

Tashkent

KIRGIZ
SSR

U R A L M O U N T A I N S

Pechora

N. Dvina

Archangel

Pechora

Sverdlovsk
(Yekaterinburg)

Perm (Molotov)

Kama

Chkalov
(Orenburg)

TADZHIK
SSR

FINLAND

Leningrad
(St Petersburg)
(Petrograd)

Gatchina

Tsarskoye Selo

Veltikiye Luki

Pskov

Nizhny Novgorod)

Gorky

Vladimir

Moscow

Ufa

Kazan

U Z B E K
SSR

Bokhara

Samarkand

Oslo

BALTIC SEA

E

L

Smolensk

Oryol

Volga

Ulyanovsk
(Simbirsk)

ARAL
SEA

AmuDarya

TURKMEN
SSR

IRAN

LIT

Minsk

Mogilyov

Kiev

Volgograd
(Tsaritsyn)
(Stalingrad)

KAZAKH STEPPES

Warsaw

Brest
Litovsk

BR

Gomel

UKRAINE

Don

Rostov-
on-Don

CASPIAN SEA

Baku

POLAND

U

Dnieper

Sevastopol

BLACK SEA

Tiflis

CAUCASUS

Batumi

AR

G

Odessa

Perekop
Isthmus

TURKEY

PERSIAN
GULF

RUMANIA

800 Mls

1200 Kms

84 Russia today.

SELECT BIBLIOGRAPHY

GENERAL WORKS

G. Barraclough, *History in a changing world* (Oxford 1955).
E. H. Carr, *1917: Before and After* (London-Melbourne-Toronto 1969).
F. Chabod, *Storia dell'idea d'Europa* (Bari 1961).
N. Ya Danilevskij, *Rossija i Evropa 1869/71*, ed. N. Strakhov (St Petersburg 1895).
W. Flitner, *Europäische* Gesittung (Zurich 1961).
M. T. Florinsky, *Russia. A History and Interpretation* (2 vols., New York 1960).
C. Goehrke, 'Geographische Grundlagen der russischen Geschichte' in *Jahrbücher für Geschichte Osteuropas*, 18 (1970).
O. Halecki, *The Limits and Divisions of European History* (London/New York 1950).
K. Jaspers, *Vom europäischen Geist*. Address, given at the Rencontres Internationales de Genève, September 1946 (Munich 1947).
H. Kohn, *Pan-Slavism. Its History and Ideology* (New York 1960).
H. Kohn (ed.), *The Mind of Modern Russia* (Rutgers, N.J. 1955).
A. G. Mazour, *Modern Russian Historiography* (Princeton 1958).
H. W. Nerhood, *To Russia and Return. An Annotated Bibliography of Travellers' English-Language Accounts of Russia from the Ninth Century to the Present* (Ohio 1969).
W. H. Parker, 'Europe: how far?' in *The Geographical Journal*, 126 (London 1960).
N. V. Riazanovsky, *Russia and the West in the Teaching of the Slavophiles* (Cambridge, Mass. 1952).
La Russie et l'Europe XVI-*XX* *siècles* (Paris-Moscow 1970). Bibliothèque générale de l'Ecole Pratique des Hautes Etudes, VI* Sect.
P. N. Savitskiy, 'La conception eurasiste de l'histoire russe' in *Résumés des communications présentés au VII* *Congrès International des sciences historiques*, II (Warsaw 1933).
D. Shapiro, *A Select Bibliography of Works in English on Russian History 1801–1917* (Oxford 1962).
V. Soloviev, 'Against the Slavophils' in *Sobranie sochineniy* (Vol. V, St. Petersburg 1911–14).
G. Stökl 'Russland und Europa vor Peter dem Grossen' in *Historische Zeitschrift*, 184/3 (December 1957).
—*Russische Geschichte von den Anfängen bis zur Gegenwart* (Stuttgart 1965)
B. H. Sumner, *Survey of Russian History* (London 1948).
— 'Russia and Europe' in *Oxford Slavonic Papers*, II (1951).

Knjaz' N. S. Trubetskoy, *Evropa i Chelovechestvo* (Sofia 1920).
D. Tschizewzkij and D. Groh (ed.), *Europa and Russland. Texte zum Problem des westeuropäischen und russischen Selbstverständnisses* (Darmstadt 1959).
P. Valéry, 'Note (ou l'Européen): Extract from a conference held at the University of Zürich 15 Nov. 1922' in *Oeuvres*, I (Paris 1957), pp. 1000–14; conf. p. 1770.
V. Weidlé, *Russia Absent and Present* (New York 1952).
K. A. Wittfogel, 'Russia and the East: A Comparison and Contrast' in *Slavic Review*, 22, 4 (December 1963); idem: Reply, l.c.; N. V. Riasanovsky: 'Oriental Despotism and Russia', l.c.

I HIDDEN EUROPE

P. Apostol, *Das Artel. Eine wirtschaftsgeschichtliche Studie* (Stuttgart 1898).
N. von Arseniev, 'Anglikanismus und Ostkirche' in *Kyrios*, I (1936).
O. P. Backus, *Motives of West Russian Nobles in Deserting Lithuania for Moscow, 1377–1514* (Lawrence, Kansas 1957).
N. de Baumgarten, 'Généalogies et mariages occidentaux des Rurikides russes du X* an XIII* siècle' in *Orientalia Christiana*, IX (Rome 1927).
Raissa Bloch, 'Verwandtschaftliche Bezeihungen des sächsischen Adels zu russischen Fürstenhäusern im 11. Jahrhundert' in *Festschrift A. Brackmann* (Berlin 1931).
J. Blum, *Lord and Peasant in Russia from the Ninth to the Nineteenth Century* (Princeton 1961).
A. A. Bogolepov, 'Church Reforms in Russia, 1905–1918' in *St Vladimir's Seminary Quarterly*, 10 (1966).
O. Brunner, 'Europäisches und russisches Bürgertum' in *Neue Wege der Verfassungs- und Sozialgeschichte* (Göttingen 1968).
M. Buber, *Pfade in Utopia* (Heidelberg 1950, cit.: p. 213).
S. Bulgakov, *The Orthodox Church* (London 1935).
H. T. Cheshire, 'The great Tartar invasion of Europe' in *Slavonic and East European Review*, 5 (1926).
S. Chetverikov, *Optina Pustyn* (Paris 1926).
S. H. Cross, 'The Scandinavian Infiltration into Early Russia' in *Speculum*, 21 (1946).
J. S. Curtiss, *Church and State in Russia. The Last Years of the Empire 1900–1917* (New York 1940).
F. Dvornik, 'The Kiev State and its Relations with Western Europe' in *Transactions of the Royal Historical Society*, 29 (London 1947).

— 'The Russia of Kiev' in *The Slavs. Their Early History and Civilization* (Boston 1956).

C. Goehrke, *Die Theorien über Entstehung und Entwicklung des 'Mir'* (Wiesbaden 1964).

B. D. Grekov, *Kievskaya Rus'* (Moscow 1953).

Sigmund Freiherr zu Herberstain, *Rerum Moscoviticarum Commentarii* (2) *1549* (Reprinted: Frankfurt a/M 1964) – English edition: *Notes upon Russia 1571* (ed. R. H. Major) (2 vols., London 1851/52).

P. Johansen, 'Novgorod und die Hanse' in *Gedächtnisschrift für Fr. Rörig* (Lübeck 1953).

W. K. Medlin, *Moscow and East Rome. A political study of the relations of Church and State in Moscovite Russia* (Geneva 1952).

I. Müller, 'Die Kritik des Protestantismus in der russischen Theologie und Philosophie' in *Die Ostkirche und die russische Christenheit* (ed. E. Benz) (Tübingen 1949).

— '*Russischer Geist und evangelisches Christentum. Die Kritik des Protestantismus in der russischen religiösen Philosophie und Dichtung im 19. und 20. Jahrhundert* (Witten/Ruhr s.a.).

Irene Neander, 'Die Bedeutung der Mongolenherrschaft in Russland' in *Geschichte in Wissenschaft und Unterricht*, 5 (1954).

H. Neubauer, *Car und Selbstherrscher, Beiträge zur Geschichte der Autokratie in Russland* (Wiesbaden 1964).

H.-H. Nolte, *Religiöse Toleranz in Russland 1600–1725* (Göttingen Philos. Diss., Göttingen-Zurich-Frankfurt 1969).

D. Obolensky, 'Russia's Byzantine Heritage' in *Oxford Slavonic Papers*, I (1950).

K. Onasch, *Ikonen* (Gütersloh 1961).

H. Schaeder, *Moskau, das Dritte Rom* (Darmstadt 1957), cf. Ja. S. Lur'e, in *Trudy Otdela drevnerusskoy literatury*, M/L 16. Bd. (1960).

H. Simon, *K.P. Pobedonostsev und die Kirchenpolitik des Heiligen Sinod 1880–1905* (Göttingen 1969).

I. Smolitsch, *Russisches Mönchtum, Entstehung, Entwicklung und Wesen 988–1917* (Würzburg 1953).

— *Leben und Lehre der Starzen* (Cologne-Olten 1958).

— *Geschichte der russischen Kirche 1700–1917*, I (Leiden 1964).

B. Spuler, 'Russia and Islam' in *Slavic Review*, 22, 4 (December 1963).

— *Die Goldene Horde. Die Mongolen in Russland 1223–1502* (Leipzig 1943).

D. Stremoukhov, 'Moscow, the Third Rome: Sources of the Doctrine' in *Speculum*, 28 (1953).

M. Szeftel, 'Joseph Volotsky's political ideas in a new historical perspective' in *Jahrbücher für Geschichte Osteuropas*, 13 (1965).

M. N. Tikhomirov, *Drevnerusskie goroda* (Moscow/Leningrad 1956).

M. N. Tikhomirov (ed.), *Novgorod.K 1100–letiju goroda. Sbornik statej* (Moscow 1964).

G. Vernadsky, *Kievan Russia* (New Haven 1951).

— *The Mongols and Russia* (New Haven 1953).

— 'Serfdom in Russia' in *Relazioni del X. Congresso Internazionale di Scienze Storiche*, 3 (Florence 1955).

— *Russia and the Dawn of the Modern Age* (Yale 1959).

II FROM MOSCOW TO ST PETERSBURG

F. von Adelung, *Kritisch-literärische Übersicht der Reisenden in Russland bis 1700, deren Berichte bekannt sind* (2 vols., St Petersburg/Leipzig 1846).

E. Amburger, *Die Familie Marselis. Studien zur russischen Wirtschaftsgeschichte* (Giessen 1957).

— *Beiträge zur Geschichte der deutsch-russischen kulturellen Beziehungen* (Giessen 1961).

— *Die Anwerbung ausländischer Fachkräfte für die Wirtschaft Russlands vom 15. bis ins 19. Jahrhundert* (Wiesbaden 1968).

M. S. Anderson, 'English views of Russia in the age of Peter the Great' in *ASEER*, 13, 2 (1954).

A. I. Andreev (ed.), *Pyotr Velikiy. Sbornik statey I* (Moscow/ Leningrad 1947).

M. Bruce, 'Jacobite relations with Peter the Great' in *SEER*, 14 (1935/36).

M. Confino, 'Histoire et psychologie: A propos de la noblesse russe au XVIIIe siècle' in *Annales* 22, 6 (November– December 1967).

E. Dvoichenko–Markov, 'William Penn and Peter the Great' in *Proceedings of the American Philosophical Society 1953*, 97, 1.

Th. Esper, 'A Sixteenth-Century anti-Russian Arms Embargo' in *Jahrbuch für Geschichte Osteuropas*, 15 (1967).

Hedwig Fleischhacker, *Die staats- und völkerrechtlichen Grundlagen der moskauischen Aussenpolitik (14.–17. Jahrhundert)* (Breslau 1938/Darmstadt 1959).

— 'Porträt Peters III' in *Jahrbücher für Geschichte Osteuropas*, 5 (1957).

Giles Fletcher, *Of the Russe Common Wealth* (ed. Works issued by the Hakluyt society; 20, 1856; p. 21).

K. Forstreuter, *Preussen und Russland von den Anfängen des Deutschen Ordens bis zu Peter dem Grossen* (Göttingen-Berlin-Frankfurt 1955).

G. von Frantzius, *Die Okkupation Ostpreussens durch die Russen im 7-jährigen Kriege mit besonderer Berücksichtigung der russischen Quellen* (Phil. Dis. Berlin 1916).

D. Gerhard, *England und der Aufstieg Russlands* (Munich/ Berlin 1933).

A. J. Gerson, 'The Organization and Early History of the Muscovy Company' in *Studies in the History of English Commerce in the Tudor Period* (University of Pennsylvania 1912).

I. Grey, 'Peter the Great in England' in *History Today*, 6 (1956).

O. Halecki, *Borderlands of Western Civilization* (New York 1952).

W. Hinz, 'Peters des Grossen Anteil an der wissenschaftlichen und künstlerischen Kultur seiner Zeit' in *Jahrbücher für Kultur und Geschichte der Slaven*, 8 (1932).

W. Leitsch, *Moskau und die Politik des Kaiserhofes im XVII. Jahrhundert, I 1604–1654* (Graz-Cologne 1960).

L. R. Lewitter, 'Peter the Great, Poland and the Westernization of Russia' in *Journal of the History of Ideas*, 19, 4 (1958).

— 'The Apocryphal Testament of Peter the Great' in *The Polish Review*, 6, 3 (1961).

F. Ley, *Le maréchal de Münnich et la Russie au XVIIIe siècle* (Paris 1959).

A. Lipski, 'A Re-examination of the "Dark Era" of Anna Ivanovna' in *ASEER*, 15 (1956).

I. Ljubimenko, 'The Struggle of the Dutch with the English for the Russian Market in the 17th Century' in *Transactions of the Royal Historical Society*, Series 4, 7 (1924).

— 'Les Relations diplomatiques de l'Angleterre avec la Russie au XVIIᵉ Siècle' in *Revue Historique*, 153 (1926).

— 'Anglo-Russian Relations during the first English Revolution' in *Transactions of the Royal Historical Society*, Series 4, 11 (1928).

Leo Loewenson, 'The First Interviews between Peter I and William III in 1697: Some Neglected English Material' in *SEER*, 36 (1957/58).

Clarence A. Manning, *Hetman of Ukraine Ivan Mazeppa* (New York 1957).

A. F. Meyendorff, 'Anglo-Russian Trade in the 16th Century' in *Slavonic and East European Review*, 25 (1946).

D. B. Miller, 'The Coronation of Ivan IV of Moscow' in *Jahrbücher für Geschichte Osteuropas*, 15 (1967).

B. Nolde, *La Formation de l'Empire Russe*, 2 vols. (Paris 1952/53).

B. Norretranders, *The Shaping of Czardom under Ivan Grozny* (Copenhagen 1964).

D. Norrman, *Gustaf Adolfs Politik mot Russland och Polen under tyska kriget (1630–1632)* (Uppsala 1943).

C. Bickford O'Brien, *Russia under two Tsars 1682–1689*, University of California, Publications in History, XLII (1952).

— *Muscovy and the Ukraine. From the Pereyaslavl agreement to the truce of Andrussovo, 1654–1667* (University of California Press, Berkeley/Los Angeles 1963).

— 'Russia and Eastern Europe. The Views of A. L. Ordin Nascokin' in *Jahrbücher für Geschichte Osteuropas*, 17 (1969).

S. F. Platonov, *Ocherki po istorii Smuty v Moskovskom Gosudarstve*, Zapiski ist.-fil.fak. St Petersburg University, 52 (St Petersburg 1899).

W. Platzhoff, 'Das erste Auftauchen Russlands und der russischen Gefahr in der europäischen Politik' in *Historische Zeitschrift*, 115 (1916).

M. Raeff, 'Home, School and Service in the Life of the 18th Century Russian Nobleman' in *Slavonic and East European Review*, 40, 95 (1962).

— *Plans for Political Reform in Imperial Russia 1730–1905* (New Jersey 1966).

— *Origins of the Russian Intelligentsia. The Eighteenth-Century Nobility* (New York 1966).

G. von Rauch, *Studien über das Verhältnis Russlands zu Europa* (Darmstadt 1964).

G. Rhode, 'Vyvod, Zwangsumsiedlungen in Osteuropa vor der Oktoberrevolution' in *Festgabe für H. Aubin* (Bonn 1951).

L. Richter, *Leibniz und sein Russlandbild* (Berlin 1946).

K.-H. Ruffmann, *Das Russlandbild im England Shakespeares* (Göttingen 1952).

— 'England und der russische Zaren- und Kaisertitel' in *Jahrbücher für Geschichte Osteuropas*, 3 (1955).

— 'Das englische Interesse am russischen Thronwechsel im Jahre 1730' in *Jahrbücher für Geschichte Osteuropas*, 5 (1957).

— 'Russischer Adel als Sondertypus der europäischen Adelswelt' in *Jahrbücher für Geschichte Osteuropas*, 9 (1961).

H. von Staden, *Aufzeichnungen über den Moskauen Staat* (ed. Fritz Epstein) (Hamburg 1930).

G. Stökl, 'Die Wurzeln des modernen Staates in Osteuropa' in *Jahrbücher für Geschichte Osteuropas*, 1 (1953).

— *Die Entstehung des Kosakentums* (Munich 1953).

B. H. Sumner, *Peter the Great and the Ottoman Empire* (Oxford 1949).

— *Peter the Great and the Emergence of Russia* (London 1950).

A. Freiherr von Taube, 'Die Livlandpolitik Ivan IV Groznyjs in der sowjetischen Geschichtsschreibung' in *Jahrbücher für Geschichte Osteuropas*, 13 (1965).

G. Tolstoy, *The first forty years of intercourse between England and Russia (1553–1593)*, Letters and Relations (St Petersburg 1875).

T. S. Willan, 'Trade between England and Russia in the second half of the XVI Century' in *English Historical Review*, 63 (1948).

E. Winter, *Halle als Ausgangspunkt der deutschen Russlandkunde im 18. Jahrhundert* (Berlin 1953).

E. Winter (ed.), *Lomonosov, Schlözer, Pallas, Deutsch-russische Wissenschaftsbeziehungen im 18. Jahrhundert* (Berlin 1962).

R. Wittram, *Peter der Grosse. Der Eintritt Russlands in die Neuzeit* (Berlin-Göttingen-Heidelberg 1954).

— *Peter I, Czar und Kaiser* (2 vols., Göttingen 1964).

M. Woltner, 'Zur Frage der Untertanenschaft von Westeuropäern in Russland bis zur Zeit Peters des Grossen einschliesslich' in *Jahrbücher für Geschichte Osteuropas*, 3. Jahrg. (1938).

S. Yakobson, 'Early Anglo-Russian Relations (1553–1613)' in *Slavonic and East European Review*, 13 (1934/35).

III EUROPEAN HEGEMONY

Erzsébet Andics, 'Das Bündnis Habsburg-Romanow. Vorgeschichte der zaristischen Intervention in Ungarn im Jahre 1849' in *Studia historica Academiae Scientiarum Hungaricae*, 52 (Budapest 1963).

R. A. Averbuch, *Tsarskaya interventsiya v bor'be s Vengerskoy revoljutsiey 1848–1849 gg.* (Moscow 1935).

P. W. Blackstock and B. F. Hoselitz, *The Russian Menace to Europe by K. Marx and F. Engels* (Glencoe, Ill. 1952).

E. H. Carr, *The Romantic Exiles* (London 1933).

J. S. Curtiss, *The Russian Army under Nicholas I, 1825–1855* (Durham, N.C. 1965).

E. I. Družinina, *Kyuchuk-Kainardzhisky mir 1774 g.* (Moscow 1955).

P. Dukes, *Catherine the Great and the Russian Nobility* (London 1967).

J. G. Gleason, *The Genesis of Russophobia in Great Britain* (Cambridge, Mass. 1950).

P. Gooch, *Catherine the Great* (London 1954).

C. de Grunwald, *La Vie de Nicolas Premier* (Paris 1946).

H.-B. Harder, *Schiller in Russland, Materialien zu einer Wirkungsgeschichte 1789–1814* (Bad Homburg v.d.H./Berlin/Zürich 1969).

171

A. Freiherr von Haxthausen, *The Russian Empire, its People, Institutions and Resources* (2 vols., London 1856).

D. B. Horn, *British Public Opinion and the First Partition of Poland* (Edinburgh 1945).

E. Hösch, 'Das sogenannte "griechische Projekt" Katharinas II' in *Jahrbücher für Geschichte Osteuropas*, 12 (1964).

Barbara Jelavich, *A Century of Russian Foreign Policy, 1814–1914* (Philadelphia/New York 1964).

H. Kallas and S. Nickels, *Finland. Creation and Construction* (London 1968).

H. H. Kaplan, *The First Partition of Poland* (New York 1962).

N. Karpovich, *Imperial Russia, 1801–1917* (New York 1932).

W. Konopczynski, 'England and the First Partition of Poland' in *Journal of Central European Affairs*, 8 (1948/9).

M. Lindemann, *Die Heiraten der Romanows und der deutschen Fürstenhäuser* (Berlin/Bonn 1935).

R. H. Lord, *The Second Partition of Poland. A Study in Diplomatic History* (Cambridge, Mass. 1915, Harvard Historical Studies 23).

A. McConnell, *A Russian 'Philosophe', Alexander Radishchev, 1749–1802* (The Hague 1964).

R. E. McGrew, 'A Political Portrait of Paul I from the Austrian and English Diplomatic Archives' in *Jahrbücher für Geschichte Osteuropas*, 18 (1970).

M. E. Malia, *Alexander Herzen and the Birth of Russian Socialism, 1812–1855* (Cambridge, Mass. 1961).

J. Ter Meulen, *Der Gedanke der Internationalen Organisation in seiner Entwicklung II, 1 (1789–1870)* (The Hague 1929).

Peter von Meyendorff, *Ein russischer Diplomat an den Höfen von Berlin und Wien. Politischer und privater Briefwechsel 1826–1863* (ed. O. Hoetzsch) (3 vols., Berlin/Leipzig 1923).

S. Monas, *The Third Section. Police and Society in Russia under Nicolas I* (Cambridge, Mass. 1961).

K. A. Papmehl, 'The Problem of Civil Liberties in the Records of the Great Commission' in *Slavonic and East European Review*, 42 (1964).

R. Portal, 'Pugatchev. Une révolution manquée' in *Etudes d'histoire moderne et contemporaine*, 1 (1947).

V. J. Puryear, *England, Russia and the Straits Question 1844–1856* (Berkeley 1931).

M. Raeff, *Michael Speransky. Statesman of Imperial Russia, 1772–1839* (The Hague 1957).

— *The Decembrist Movement* (New Jersey 1966).

N. V. Riazanovsky, *Nicholas I and Official Nationality in Russia 1825–1855* (University of California Press, Berkeley 1959).

G. Sacke, *Die Gesetzgebende Kommission Katherinas II* (Breslau 1940).

Sbornik imperatorskago russkago istoricheskago obshchestva, X, 1872: letters of Catherine II, pp. 176, 351, 411, 504; XII, 1873: report of Henry Shirley.

Hildegard Schaeder, *Autokratie und Heilige Allianz* (Darmstadt 1963).

P. Scheibert, *Von Bakunin zu Lenin* (Leiden 1956).

A. von Schelting, *Russland und Europa im russischen Geschichtsdenken* (Berne 1948).

H. Seton-Watson, *The Russian Empire 1801–1917* (London 1967).

L. I. Strakhovsky, *Alexander I of Russia* (London 1947).

M. M. Shtrange, *Russkoye obshchestvo i frantsuzskaya revoljutsiya 1789–1794* (Moscow 1956).

B. H. Sumner, 'New Material on the Revolt of Pugachev' in *Slavonic and East European Review*, 7 (1928/29).

E. V. Tarle, *Krymskaya voyna* (2 vols., Moscow/Leningrad 1950).

G. S. Thomson, *Catherine the Great and the Expansion of Russia* (London 1947).

H.-J. Torke, 'Das russische Beamtentum in der 1. Hälfte des 19. Jahrhunderts' in *Forschungen zur osteuropäischen Geschichte*, 13 (Berlin 1967).

D. Tschizewskij (ed.), *Hegel bei den Slaven* (Darmstadt 1964).

R. Wittram, *Baltische Geschichte. Grundzüge und Durchblicke* (Munich 1954).

— 'Das russische Imperium und sein Gestaltwandel' in *Historische Zeitschrift*, 187/3 (1959).

L. Yaresh, 'The "Peasant Wars" in Soviet Historiography' in *Slavonic and East European Review*, 16 (1957).

V. Graf Zubow, *Zar Paul I. Mensch und Schicksal* (Stuttgart 1963).

IV THE ASIAN HORIZON: COLONIAL POWER – WORLD POWER

D. Y. Dallin, *The Rise of Russia in Asia* (New York 1963).

J. Glazik, *Die russisch-orthodoxe Heidenmission seit Peter dem Grossen* (Münster i. W. 1954).

— *Die Islammission der russisch-orthodoxen Kirche* (Münster i. W. 1959).

F. A. Golder, 'The Purchase of Alaska' in *American Historical Review*, 25 (1919/20).

— *Russian Expansion on the Pacific 1641–1850* (Cleveland 1914).

W. Habberton, 'Anglo-Russian Relations concerning Afghanistan, 1837–1907' (*Illinois Studies in the Social Sciences*, 21, 1937).

O. Hoetzsch, *Russland in Asien. Geschichte einer Expansion* (Stuttgart 1967).

E. Hölzle, *Russland und Amerika* (Munich 1953).

Istoriya Sibiri s drevneyshikh vremen do nashich dney v 5 tomakh (Leningrad 1968).

N. M. Jadrintsev, *Sibir' kak koloniya v geograficheskom, etnograficheskom i istoricheskom otnoshenii* (St Petersburg 1892).

G. Kennan, *Siberia and the Exile System* (2 vols., London 1891).

G. V. Lantzeff, *Siberia in the 17th Century* (University of California Publications in History, XXX, Berkeley 1943).

A. Malozemoff, *Russian Far Eastern Policy 1881–1904* (Berkeley/Los Angeles 1958).

S. B. Okun, *The Russian-American Company* (Cambridge, Mass. 1951).

R. A. Pierce (ed.), *Mission to Turkestan. Being the memoirs of Count K. K. Pahlen, 1908–1909* (London 1964).

— *Russian Central Asia 1867–1917* (Berkeley 1960).

M. Raeff, *Siberia and the Reforms of 1822* (Seattle, Washington 1956).

B. H. Sumner, 'Tsardom and Imperialism in the Far East and Middle East, 1880–1914' in *Proceedings of the British Academy* (1941; p. 27).

G. Vernadsky, 'The Expansion of Russia' in *Transactions of the Connecticut Academy of arts and sciences*, **31** (1933).

H. de Windt, *The New Siberia* (London 1896).

E. H. Zabriskie, *American-Russian Rivalry in the Far East . . . , 1895–1914* (Philadelphia 1946).

S. V. Zhukovsky, *Snosheniya Rossii s Bukharoy i Khivoy za poslednee trechsotletye* (Petrograd 1915).

V RUSSIA IN THE EUROPEAN POWER SYSTEM

W. M. Carlgren, *Iswolsky und Aehrenthal vor der bosnischen Annexionskrise: Russische und österreich-ungarische Balkanpolitik 1906–1908* (Uppsala 1955).

A. Dallin (ed.), *Russian Diplomacy and Eastern Europe 1914–1917* (New York 1963).

S. Goriainov, *Le Bosphore et les Dardanelles* (Paris 1910).

— *La Question d'Orient à la veille du Traité de Berlin 1870–1878, d'après les archives russes* (Paris 1948).

W. W. Gottlieb, *Studies in Secret Diplomacy during the First World War* (London 1957).

O. Hauser, 'Die englisch-russische Konvention von 1907 und die Meerengenfrage' in *Festschrift für Otto Becker* (Wiesbaden 1954).

H. Heilbronner, 'Aehrenthal in Defense of Russian Autocracy' in *Jahrbücher für Geschichte Osteuropas*, **17** (1969).

Gisela Hünigen, *N. P. Ignat'ev und die russische Balkanpolitik 1875–1878* (Göttingen, Zürich, Frankfurt 1968).

Ch. and B. Jelavich, *Russia in the East, 1876–1880 (. . . through the letters of A. G. Jomini to N. K. Giers)* (Leiden 1959).

A. Junk, *Die Mächte auf der ersten Haager Friedenskonferenz (1898)* (Phil. Diss. Frankfurt a.M. 1929).

K. Krupinski, 'Russland und Japan. Ihre Beziehungen bis zum Frieden von Portsmouth' in *Osteuropäische Forschungen*, **27** (1939).

I. J. Lederer (ed.), *Russian Foreign Policy: Essays in Historical Perspective* (New Haven/London 1962).

A. Leroy-Beaulieu, *L'Empire des Tsars et les Russes* (2 vols., Paris 1881/82; 3 vols., 1897/98).

W. N. Medlicott, *The Congress of Berlin and after, 1878–1880* (London 1938).

— 'Bismarck and the Three Emperors Alliance 1881–1887' in *Transactions of the Royal Historical Society*, Series 4, **27** (1945).

W. E. Mosse, *Alexander II and the Modernization of Russia* (New York 1962).

— *The European Powers and the German Question 1848–1871 with special reference to England and Russia* (Cambridge, Mass. 1958).

B. Nolde, *L'Alliance Franco-russe* (Paris 1936).

M. B. Petrovich, *The Emergence of Russian Panslavism 1856–1870* (New York 1956).

P. Renouvin, 'Les relations franco-russes à la fin du XIXe et au début du XXe siècle. Bilan des recherches' in *Cahiers du monde russe et soviétique*, **1** (May 1959).

W. A. Renzi, 'Great Britain, Russia, and the Straits, 1914–1915' in *The Journal of Modern History*, **42**, 1 (March 1970).

R. A. Romanov, *Ocherki diplomaticheskoy istorii russko-yaponskoy voyny (1895–1907)* (Moscow/Leningrad 1955).

B. Ropponen, *Die Kraft Russlands. Wir beurteilte die politische und militärische Führung der europäischen Grossmächte in der Zeit von 1905 bis 1914 die Kraft Russlands* (Helsinki 1968).

C. Jay Smith, Jr, *The Russian Struggle for Power 1914–1917. A Study of Russian Foreign Policy during the First World War* (New York 1956).

B. H. Sumner, *Russia and the Balkans 1870–1880* (Oxford 1937).

M. A. Taube, *La politique russe d'avantguerre et la fin de l'empire des tsars, 1904–1917* (Paris 1928).

E. C. Thaden, *Conservative Nationalism in Nineteenth-Century Russia* (Seattle, Washington 1964).

— *Russia and the Balkan Alliance of 1912* (Pennsylvania 1965).

Sir Donald Mackenzie Wallace, *Russia* (London 1877).

R. Wittram, 'Die russisch-nationalen Tendenzen der achtziger Jahre im Spiegel der österreichisch-ungarischen diplomatischen Berichte aus St. Petersburg' in *Kaehler-Festschrift* (Düsseldorf 1950).

— 'Bismarck und Gortčakov im Mai 1875' in *Nachrichten der Akademie der Wissenschaften in Göttingen*, **1** Phil.-Hist. Kl. 1955, No. 7.

— 'Bismarck und Russland' in W. Markert (ed.) *Deutsch-russische Beziehungen von Bismarck bis zur Gegenwart* (Stuttgart 1964).

VI AN OPEN EUROPE

P. L. Alston, *Education and The State in Tsarist Russia* (Stanford 1969).

C. E. Black (ed.), *The Transformation of Russian Society* (Cambridge, Mass. 1960).

Sophie Brutzer, *Rilkes russische Reisen* (Phil. Diss. Königsberg Pr. 1935).

H. Dahm, *Vladimir Soloviev und Max Scheler – ein Beitrag zur Geschichte der Phänomenologie* (Munich 1970).

M. Doerne, *Tolstoj und Dostojewskij. Zwei christliche Utopien* (Göttingen 1969).

S. M. Dubrovskii, *Stolypinskaya zemelnaya reforma* (Moscow 1963).

T. Emmons, *The Russian Landed Gentry and the Peasant Emancipation of 1861* (London 1968).

G. Fischer, *Russian Liberalism: From Gentry to Intelligentsia* (Cambridge, Mass. 1958).

I. Getzler, *Martov. A political biography of a Russian Social Democrat* (London/New York 1967).

D. Geyer, *Lenin in der russischen Sozialdemokratie* (Cologne/Graz 1962).

— *Die Russische Revolution. Historische Probleme und Perspektiven* (Stuttgart 1968).

Russlands Aufbruch ins 20. Jahrhundert: Politik-Gesellschaft-Kultur 1894–1917 (ed. G. Katkov, E. Oberländer, N. Poppe, G. von Rauch) (Olten und Freiburg i. Br. 1970).

J. L. H. Keep, *The Rise of Social Democracy in Russia* (Oxford 1963).

Th. H. von Laue, *Sergei Witte and the Industrialization of Russia* (New York/London 1963).

C. L. Lundin, 'The Road from Tsar to Kaiser: Changing Loyalties of the Baltic Germans, 1905–1914' in *Journal of Central European Affairs*, **10**, 3 (1950).

P.J. Lyashchenko, *History of the National Economy of Russia to the 1917 Revolution* (New York 1953).

A. Meyendorff, *The Background of the Russian Revolution* (New York 1931. Index and Errata 1942).

H. Meynell, 'The Stockholm Conference of 1917' in *International Review of Social History*, **5** (1960).

Margaret Miller, *The Economic Development of Russia 1905–1914* (New York 1967).

D.S. Mirskij, *A History of Russian Literature* (New York 1960).

J. Nötzold, *Wirtschaftspolitische Alternativen der Entwicklung Russlands in der Ara Witte und Stolypin* (Berlin/Munich 1966).

A. Rabinovitch, *Prelude to Revolution: The Petrograd Bolsheviks and the July 1917 Uprising* (Bloomington, Ind. 1968).

O.H. Radkey, *The Election of the Russian Constituent Assembly of 1917* (Harvard Historical Monograms 21, Cambridge, Mass. 1950).

— 'Chernov and Agrarian Socialism before 1918' in *Continuity and Change in Russian and Soviet Thought*, ed. J. Simmons (Cambridge, Mass. 1955).

— *The Agrarian Foes of Bolshevism. Promise and Default of the Russian Socialist Revolutionaries February to October 1917* (New York 1958).

Thomas Riha, *A Russian European. Paul Miliukov in Russian Politics* (International Studies of the Committee on International Relations, University of Notre Dame, Indiana 1969).

G.T. Robinson, *Rural Russia under the Old Regime. A history of the landlord-peasant world and a prologue to the peasant revolution of 1917* (New York 1949).

H. Rothfels, 'Reich, Staat und Nation im deutsch-baltischen Denken' in *Schriften der Königsberger Gelehrten Gesellschaft, Geisteswissenschaftl.* Kl. 7, Jahr Heft 4 (1930).

H. Seton-Watson, *The Decline of Imperial Russia* (London/New York 1952).

S.R. Tompkins, *The Russian Intelligentsia Makers of the Revolutionary State* (Norman, Oklahoma 1957).

A.B. Ulam, *Lenin and the Bolsheviks. The Intellectual and the Political History of the Triumph of Communism in Russia* (London 1966).

F. Venturi, *Il Populismo Russo* (Turin 1952). English edition: *Roots of Revolution. A History of the Populist and Socialist Movements in 19th century Russia* (London 1960).

B. Veselovskij, *Istoriya zemstva za sorok let* (4 vols., St Petersburg 1909/11).

P. Vinogradoff, *Self-Government in Russia* (London 1915).

R.D. Warth, *The Allies and the Russian Revolution* (Durham, N.C. 1954).

C. Williams, 'Russians in Germany 1900–1914' in *Journal of Temporary History*, **1** (1966).

R. Wittram, 'Das Freiheitsproblem in der russischen inneren Geschichte' in *Jahrbücher für Geschichte Osteuropas*, **2** (1954).

— 'Studien zum Selbstverständnis des 1. und 2. Kabinetts der russischen Provisorischen Regierung (März bis Juli 1917), in *Abhandlungen der Akademie der Wissenschaften in Göttingen*, Phil.-Hist. Kl. III, 78 (1971).

Z.A.B. Zeman, *Germany and the Revolution in Russia, 1915–1918. Documents from the Archives of the German Foreign Ministry* (London 1958).

V. Zenkovsky, *A History of Russian Philosophy* (2 vols., New York 1953).

ILLUSTRATION CREDITS

INDEX